Praise for *Content – The Atomic Particle of Marketing*

D0770288

'Content strategy has become marketing's darling, and with its arrival comes a chorus of pundits and gurus attempting to define it and counsel brands mired in overwhelm and confusion. Out of that chaos comes Rebecca Lieb's clear and logical voice. She's more than the analyst who has spent the most time researching her topic – she's also a marketer, author and an editor who has run newsrooms. To understand content marketing bottom-up, top-down and inside-out, read this book.' **Stephanie Losee, Head of Content, Visa**

'The high priestess of digital marketing and media, Rebecca Lieb, channels her wisdom into the most comprehensive book on the complex topic of content marketing. This book is the strategic big bang that marketers can't afford to miss.' **Jason Miller, Global Content Marketing Leader, LinkedIn Marketing Solutions**

'The majority of global marketers have no discernable content marketing strategy. With this book, they have no more excuses.' **Joe Pulizzi, Founder, Content Marketing Institute, and author of *Content Inc* and *Epic Content Marketing***

'Based on years of research and hands-on client engagement, Rebecca Lieb has created the one-stop guide to everything that you need to know to be successful at content marketing. Buy copies for yourself and each member of your team to ensure that you are all on the same page with these best practices.' **Charlene Li, Principal Analyst, Altimeter, a Prophet Company, and author of *The Engaged Leader* and *Open Leadership*, co-author of *Groundswell***

'Rebecca Lieb understands what so many marketers and business leaders are struggling to grasp in today's digital world – that content is the only way to find new customers, but also to retain employees and build business success. Content is so central to business growth today that it truly is the "atomic particle" of marketing and innovation.' **Michael Brenner, globally recognized keynote speaker, author of *The Content Formula* and CEO of Marketing Insider Group**

'*Content – The Atomic Particle of Marketing* should be required reading for any role holder with a 'C' in their acronym. If you are trying to drive content and digital transformation in your organization, Rebecca Lieb's book will absolutely weaponize you with frameworks and industry examples to support successful integration of content marketing and strategy into your growth and transformational activities. The comprehensive landscape offered within this book is not just for marketers – it's essential reading for those in any organization needing to navigate the many perils of 21st-century relationship management. It will help you rise above the noise and deliver real relevance to real people, in support of goals and objectives, at scale, globally. No one surpasses Rebecca Lieb's breadth and depth of understanding of content as practised today (I've checked). Do not hesitate to avail yourself of the years of research and compressed wisdom contained herein.' **Carlos Abler, Content Marketing Strategy Leader, 3M**

'If content is the atomic particle of marketing, Rebecca Lieb is a quantum physicist. She has, once again, deftly articulated the imperative for content as a strategic function in the enterprise. If you're looking for the foundational elements of a content marketing strategy, you can stop. You've found it here.' **Robert Rose, Chief Strategy Adviser, The Content Marketing Institute**

'In deconstructing marketing to the atomic level, Rebecca Lieb has penned an essential guide to forces that are continually reshaping how businesses attract and retain customers. Professionals at all levels will learn from her frameworks, formulas and countless examples that elucidate both the science and art of content marketing.' **David Berkowitz, Chief Strategy Officer, Sysomos**

'As a veteran content marketer constantly looking for the best insights in the industry, I've always found immense value in Rebecca Lieb's unique point of view. She is at the forefront of the latest trends and opportunities in content marketing. Her insight goes well beyond observation and gets into the tangible application of her cutting-edge research and how it can drive your efforts as a content marketer to new levels.' **Luke Kintigh, Head of Publishing, Intel iQ**

'This is a must-read for anyone working with content marketing – old pros as well as beginners. Rebecca Lieb provides us with useful insights and tools on everything from strategy and processes to distribution and measurements. The book makes for both an inspiring read and a practical guide to keep handy.' **Pontus Staunstrup, Content Marketing Strategist, Staunstrup**

'Rebecca Lieb has a masterful understanding of people, trends and ideas that move marketing forward. With *Content – The Atomic Particle of Marketing* she makes the content marketing revolution easy to understand and impossible to deny.' **Jeffrey K Rohrs, CMO, Yext, and author, *Audience: Marketing in the age of subscribers, fans & followers***

'From understanding the importance of – and difference between – Content Strategy and Content Marketing Strategy to Real-Time and Contextual Marketing, *Content – The Atomic Particle of Marketing* is a manifesto for how to succeed with content marketing now and into the future with the IoT and artificial intelligence. I love the way Lieb connects the dots!' **Ardath Albee, author, *Digital Relevance***

'Long ago Rebecca Lieb was our editor at ClickZ. We built a great business based on content marketing and Rebecca helped us along the way. In these days of newly minted content marketing "experts" it's refreshing to read a comprehensive guide from someone who has the credentials
expert. We recommend you read this book. It's truly
to content marketing strategy.' **Bryan and Jeffrey
egends.com, authors, *Be Like Amazon: Even a
n do it* and *New York Times* bestsellers *Call To Action
ur Cat To Bark?***

'There is a reason so few companies get content marketing strategy right: it's hard. This book is just what everybody has been waiting for – it's insightful, intelligent, inspiring, structured and generous – just like Rebecca Lieb herself. If you only have time to read one book this year choose this one!' **Jesper Laursen, CEO, Brand Movers**

'Rebecca Lieb is a rare sane voice in an industry noisy with hype. *Content – The Atomic Particle of Marketing* simultaneously cuts through the B.S. and teaches marketers exactly how they need to think to succeed in content. In a word, it's brilliant.' **Shane Snow, Co-founder, Contently**

Content – The Atomic Particle of Marketing

The definitive guide to content marketing strategy

Rebecca Lieb
with Jaimy Szymanski

KoganPage

First published in Great Britain and the United States in 2017 by Kogan Page Limited

2nd Floor, 45 Gee Street	c/o Martin P Hill Consulting	4737/23 Ansari Road
London	122 W 27th St, 10th Floor	Daryaganj
EC1V 3RS	New York, NY 10001	New Delhi 110002
United Kingdom	USA	India

www.koganpage.com

ISBN   978 0 7494 7975 6
E-ISBN   978 0 7494 7976 3

British Library Cataloguing-in-Publication Data

A CIP record for this book is available from the British Library.

Library of Congress Cataloging-in-Publication Data
Names: Lieb, Rebecca, author. | Szymanski, Jaimy, author.
Title: Content, the atomic particle of marketing : the definitive guide to
   content marketing strategy / Rebecca Lieb with Jaimy Szymanski.
Description: 1st Edition. | New York : Kogan Page Ltd, [2017] | Includes
   bibliographical references and index. | Description based on print version
   record and CIP data provided by publisher; resource not viewed.
Identifiers: LCCN 2017010381 (print) | LCCN 2017011267 (ebook) | ISBN
   9780749479763 (ebook) | ISBN 9780749479756 (alk. paper) | ISBN 9780749479763
   (eISBN)
Subjects: LCSH: Internet marketing. | Online social networks.
Classification: LCC HF5415.1265 (ebook) | LCC HF5415.1265 .L54 2017 (print) |
   DDC 658.8/02–dc23

Typeset by Integra Software Services, Pondicherry
Print production managed by Jellyfish
Printed and bound by CPI Group (UK) Ltd, Croydon, CR0 4YY

CONTENTS

ABOUT THE AUTHOR

As an industry analyst, Rebecca Lieb has published the largest body of research on content marketing, content strategy and content's role in the intersection of paid, owned and earned media (see http://rebeccalieb.com/research).

Lieb has followed digital marketing since its inception. In addition to senior global marketing roles at major media companies (including German network RTL Television and Universal Television and Networks Group) as well as start-ups, she has headed some of the major trade publications covering digital marketing and advertising, including the ClickZ Network, Search Engine Watch and Econsultancy's US operations.

She is a frequent public speaker on topics related to digital marketing, advertising and media (see more at http://rebeccalieb.com/speaking).

As a strategic adviser, Rebecca works with many of the world's leading brands on digital marketing innovation. Her clients range from start-up to non-profits to Fortune 100 brands and regulated industries, including Facebook, Home Depot, Nestlé, Anthem, Adobe, Honeywell, DuPont, Fidelity, Gannett, IBM, New York Life, Anthem Blue Cross, Save the Children, Pinterest, Cisco, ad and PR agencies, and the Federal Reserve Bank of New York.

She has written two previous books: *The Truth About Search Engine Optimization* instantly became an Amazon best-seller and *Content Marketing* was one of the first books on that topic.

PREFACE

Ten years ago, the extra magic ingredient was search. Before that, it was e-mail. For the past five years or so, social media has been the de rigueur term to describe marketing product and services offerings.

Suddenly, all that is changing again. Marketing can't be cutting edge in the digital sphere unless it's connected to the word 'content'.

This is both good news and bad news for those of us who have been preaching the content gospel for years (even before – and during – the whole search thing). Suddenly (suddenly?), content matters. It has taken centre stage. It is noticed, acknowledged – and important. That's the good part.

What's the bad? With attention and a bit of notoriety comes backlash. Backlash is inevitable. It's human nature. It happens with celebrities, health fads, diets, fashion and whatever is at the vanguard of digital marketing and technology.

Even a *New York Times* op-ed decried the term in 2013:

> The first time I ever heard the word 'content' used in its current context, I understood that all my artist friends and I – henceforth, 'content providers' – were essentially extinct. This contemptuous coinage is predicated on the assumption that it's the delivery system that matters, relegating what used to be called 'art' – writing, music, film, photography, illustration – to the status of filler, stuff to stick between banner ads.[1]

Hate the word if you want to, but it's still easier to say 'content' than to say 'writing and music and film and photography and illustration', not to mention 'video and charts and infographics and audio and other media'.

Rachel Lovinger at Razorfish blogged a very apt response in 2013:

> Hating on the word 'content' is like a chef saying 'I don't make food. Food is what people get at McDonald's.' Well, there probably are chefs who feel that way, but it's based on a fallacy. At the same time, I would never, ever refer to my favourite chef as a 'food maker'. The word 'content' isn't perfect, but I don't want to see it vilified. We need words to be able to talk about these principles and practices.[2]

Honestly, I don't care if you call it content or not (but do let me know if you come up with something better). What matters is... why it matters.

Here is why content matters:

Content is the atomic particle of all digital marketing. Everything. There is no owned media without content. There's no social media without content. And there's no paid media without content. And there's certainly no media-media, as in actual digital publications, without content. Pushing back even earlier, when you search, you are searching for content. Even e-mail marketing, once the darling of the digital arsenal, now relegated to wallpaper status (but still critically important), is a container for... you guessed it: content.

In advertising they call it 'creative', but that is just another term for the content that fills squares and rectangles, as well as broadcast segments.

Content is seminal. I believe the reason it is getting all this attention (let the haters hate) is the growing realization of how much it actually matters.

There is a surge of industry momentum around content now, too. Adobe confirmed it will merge its Creative Cloud Suite (PhotoShop, Illustrator, everything needed to publish digitally) with its Marketing Cloud, everything you need to advertise (and measure) in display and social media. Oracle has been acquiring tools like content marketing start-up Compendium. Oracle also snapped up Eloqua. The big guns of digital marketing, advertising and customer relationship management (CRM) are suddenly, blazingly, coming to the realization that content is what makes all that marketing possible.

Perhaps you will never derive contentment from the word 'content'. But it is high time to give the concept a second thought. Because really, isn't content the alpha and omega of everything you have ever done in digital (or any other kind of) marketing?

Notes

1 Kreider, T (2013) [accessed January 2017] Slaves of the Internet, Unite!, *The New York Times* [Online] http://www.nytimes.com/2013/10/27/opinion/sunday/slaves-of-the-internet-unite.html?_r=1

2 Lovinger, R (2013) [accessed January 2017] The Trouble with Content Part 1, *Razorfish* [Online] http://scattergather.razorfish.com/1401/2013/10/29/the-trouble-with-content-part-1/

ACKNOWLEDGEMENTS

This book is a compendium of a body of research, and research cannot be conducted without a host of keenly intelligent and generous collaborators.

Gratitude is due first and foremost to the dozens of marketing executives who gave so selflessly of their time and insights in long, probing interviews for no other reason than to help move their industry forward. All are busy people with demanding responsibilities who nevertheless made the time to share their progresses and pitfalls, opinions and experience.

Thanks are also due to my clients. Research is a key element of client engagements. Making strategic recommendations for content and other components of digital marketing strategy can only be done following a deep discovery process, which entails interviews with dozens of stakeholders from across the organization. These discussions with not only marketers but members of IT departments, corporate communications, creative staff, divisional and regional leads, all inform how content can be socialized, circulated and evangelized, and promoted across the entirety of an organization, be it a start-up, non-profit, agency, regulated industry or Fortune 50 conglomerate.

My research partners also played a critical role, particularly my former colleagues at Altimeter Group, the source of much of this research. Charlene Li led that company and kindly cooperated with the writing of this book. My fellow analysts, particularly Brian Solis and Jeremiah Owyang, gave generously of their own research findings and contacts (Jeremiah was also my co-author on the research that serves as the foundation of Chapter 3, on converged media). Susan Etlinger helped invaluably as co-author on content metrics research.

Jessica Groopman deserves special mention as the researcher with whom I worked hand-in-glove on much of the material in this book. So too does Jaimy Szymanski, another research partner extraordinaire and also the person with whom I directly collaborated on this book. Without Jaimy's help and thoughtful contributions, this book could not have happened.

Finally, deepest gratitude to my most tireless champion and supporter, my sweetie Robert Dennis.

The shift to content marketing

We're tuning out the noise.

Today's consumer lives in a virtual Times Square of messaging. A plethora of screens (televisions, PCs, tablets, watches, mobile phones), billboards, and print and broadcast media almost literally scream for attention 24/7. The more channels and media we introduce into our lives the louder and more incessant the din.

Consumers are bombarded with a never-ending stream of 'push' messaging; advertising, the marketing of interruption, of insistence and of distraction. The louder the hue and cry, the less effectively it works. Interactive media make it possible for consumers to control more of the conversation, to block out the noise and to accept only 'pull' messaging: the content they want and need, when they want and need it.

This is the overarching trend that sets the stage for content marketing's meteoric ascendance over the past decade. Content marketing is hardly new. Brands have been publishing newsletters and other forms of content for centuries. The democratization that technology affords content production literally puts the ability to be a publisher or a broadcaster in everyone's hand (or pocket).

But now that advertising effectiveness is in steep decline, marketing practitioners must inevitably turn to other forms of marketing to better engage customers during their digital journey. Content marketing (and its underlying strategy) have emerged as dominant in the new marketing hierarchy as brands seek alternatives to paid media marketing that no longer produces tangible or measureable-enough business results.

Changing customer attitudes toward advertising, combined with data privacy concerns and increased use of new mobile technologies, also contribute to advertising's steady decline. When marketers focus instead on content needs and expectations at each stage of the customer journey, they are rewarded with new opportunities for engagement, sales and retention. These opportunities are also easier to measure, offering still more incentive for marketers to focus on content in lieu of their incumbent advertising strategies.

This chapter explores why marketers should build customer-centric marketing strategies that rely more on valuable content and less on media buys. By creating a solid content strategy foundation, investing across the customer journey, realigning the marketing mix accordingly, and building the right team, digital marketers can achieve demonstrable results that span far beyond click-through rates and brand awareness.

The rise of digital, mobile and social technologies has transformed traditional advertising into a commodity, floating in a sea of media buy options and more relevant marketing investments. Advertising was once the 'boss' of marketing channels and tactics because it cost the most. Now, brands respond to new customer expectations with relevant content at every stage of their purchase decision journey. Sophisticated marketers are exploring other marketing avenues that offer greater control, while advertising remains costly even as returns diminish.

Moreover, today's consumer is both banner-blind and blocking online ads altogether. Click-through rates on standard banner ads plummeted to 0.12 per cent in 2014,[1] as customers demand more engaging and timely brand experiences (Figure 1.1).

The battle for consumer attention has never been fiercer, or more difficult. With the increased utilization of browser plug-ins that block ads from ever loading onto a screen, it is estimated that 12 per cent of display ads are never seen by humans,[2] translating into US $18.5 billion in ad-spend waste in 2015 alone.[3] Separate from ad-blocker usage, consumers subconsciously ignore digital advertising, with 60 per cent suffering 'banner blindness', meaning that they are unable to recall any of the online banner ads they are exposed to.[4]

Figure 1.1   Search for 'ad blocker' on Google Trends

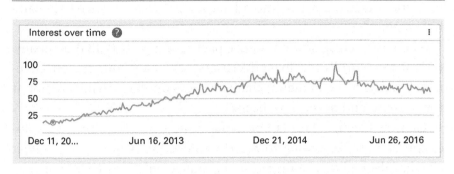

SOURCE Google (2016) https://www.google.com/trends/explore?q=%22ad%20blocker%22

Add to these facts that 94 per cent of online video viewers skip pre-roll ads before the five-second mark,[5] and 25 per cent of the video ad views are fraudulent,[6] and marketers can no longer ignore the need to shift their marketing spend away from traditional tactics towards more engaging content deployments.

Fake news is a newer trend affecting both brand and consumer attitudes to media. The disinformation trend emerged sharply during the contentious 2016 US presidential election. Brands were aghast to find their ads positioned next to fake and often sensationalistic and incendiary stories. Consumer trust in those brands is, of course, negatively impacted by these types of adjacencies.

Digital consumers are not the only ones to blame for declining advertising effectiveness. The ever-increasing level of automation in programmatic digital advertising, combined with an increase in programmatic spend[7] (even as rate card prices plummet), has further depleted effectiveness in favour of a 'set it and forget it' mentality among many practitioners.

Additionally, a lack of transparency from ad and media agencies regarding online advertising spending and effectiveness has eroded relations between some of them and the brands they represent. In October 2015, the Association of National Advertisers went as far as to engage former FBI agents to investigate suspect agency practices.[8] Major advertiser Kraft Foods has also publicly declared its rejection of up to 85 per cent of all impressions offered by real-time ad marketplaces.[9] In December 2016 the United States Department of Justice opened a probe into ad agency production price fixing and bid-rigging.

The media chief of a consumer packaged goods (CPG) company, one of the world's top-five advertisers, also questions the effectiveness of advertising in digital channels: 'Ads on the internet are not fit for purpose and never have been.'

General Electric (GE) is not alone in its marketing budget reallocation choices. According to a 2015 IBM/CMO Club study, content clinched the majority of the marketing budget at 13 per cent, trailed by digital advertising at 11 per cent; traditional advertising at 11 per cent; and analogue physical activities at 11 per cent.[10]

When advertising budgets are increased, it is most often in support of social media or mobile marketing advertising, as is the case with Johnson & Johnson (J&J). Gail Horwood, vice president (VP) of Worldwide Digital Strategy, reports that J&J is doubling social media ad spending in 2016, but not allocating more to traditional online display advertising. Native advertising and other forms of converged media are also seeing a larger share of brand budgets (though from available survey data on types of media spend it is impossible to assess how much).

Content budgets are on the rise and are predicted to continue to increase: 51 per cent of business-to-business (B2B) marketers and 50 per cent of business-to-consumer (B2C) marketers plan to increase content marketing spending over the next year, according to the Content Marketing Institute's 2016 benchmark report (see Figures 1.2 and 1.3).[11] The same study also shows those same marketers rank banner ads as the least effective form of paid promotion.

Jeremiah Glodoveza, formerly of Avaya, a technology solutions provider for team engagement, agrees that brands too joined the fray in blotting out ads. 'We've seen failed expectations with traditional advertising. At Avaya we spent a lot on traditional advertising – outdoor, sponsorships, online, print – and we saw no correlation between this increase in spend and any quantifiable marketing metric. At least when we shifted to native and digital we were able to see impact – positive and negative.'

Figure 1.2 Global content marketing revenues rose 13.3 per cent in 2014 to $26.47 billion, and expected to post a compound annual growth rate of 15.4 per cent to $54.25 billion by 2019

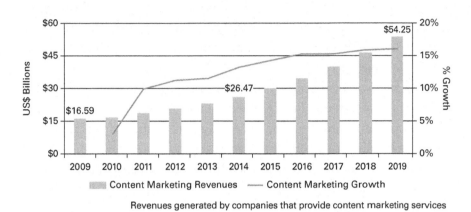

Revenues generated by companies that provide content marketing services

SOURCE PQ Media Global Content Marketing Forecast 2015–19 [Online] http://www.pqmedia.com/gcmf-2015-2019.html

Figure 1.3 When in-house spending included; global content marketing $145 billion industry, growing to over $313 billion in 2019

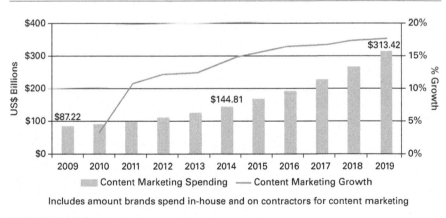

Includes amount brands spend in-house and on contractors for content marketing

SOURCE PQ Media

This advertising adverse trend is hardly limited to digital channels. GE's Chief Marketing Officer Linda Boff recently announced that the company is pulling back from television advertising, excepting live and tentpole events such as the Academy Awards or Super Bowl, due to fragmented consumer attention and a lack of engagement. Meanwhile, the company has doubled down on content marketing initiatives, particularly in digital channels.[12]

Though advertising fraud and lack of online engagement contribute to the shift from advertising to more content-based marketing, they are not the sole driving forces. As digital evolves, so, too, do a plethora of messaging platforms, as well as where, when and how those messages can be delivered. Upstart Snapchat snagged $70 million in spend from WPP alone in 2016, announced Chief Executive Officer (CEO) George Sorrel.

Marketers must therefore shift focus to content, the 'fuel' of the marketing ecosystem, and away from paid channels (see Figure 1.4). This creates a foundation for delivering right-time, relevant messaging to customers, regardless of platform.

Additional factors spurring the shift from advertising to content include:

Attitudinal

Consumers dislike and mistrust online ads: 30 per cent report online advertising is not effective, and 54 per cent believe web banner ads don't work.[13] Adding adjectives to injury, more than half of consumers apply terms such as 'annoying', 'distracting' and 'invasive' to desktop and mobile web ads, according to the same Adobe study.

Figure 1.4   Content Marketing Job Growth on Indeed.com

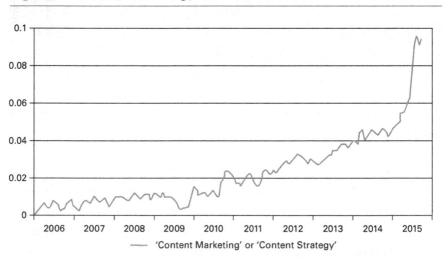

'Content Marketing' or 'Content Strategy'

SOURCE Fractl/Moz Report (2015) [Online] https://moz.com/blog/the-inbound-marketing-economy

Privacy and safety

TrustE reports that one in four consumers worry about the security or privacy of the data collected on smart devices, and only 20 per cent believe the benefits of smart devices outweigh these concerns.[14] They are also concerned about malware attacks and location-specific surveillance.

Channel and platform proliferation

New social platforms and converged media formats, like hybrid native advertising, challenge marketers to create not only more content than ever before, but also content that can be easily adapted. It is more challenging (and complex) to manufacture content that fits paid, owned, earned and converged media channels than it is to focus solely on advertising.

Marketers today find it increasingly necessary to invest in multiple channels to avoid risk, as efficacy typically waxes and wanes between channels and platforms. Experimenting with new channels can pay off though, as Unilever found that buzz derived from its social content was significantly driving sales. This resulted in the company investing 'tens of millions' more into its social presence.[15]

Mobile

As mobile overtakes not only desktop computing but also television in media consumption hours spent,[16] marketers are increasingly challenged by the decrease of advertising 'real estate' on devices' smaller screens. Mobile's intrinsically personal nature also makes interruptive forms of advertising seem all the more invasive. Additionally, there is an escalating cost to consumers, as mobile advertising becomes bandwidth intensive, eating into data plans more than opt-in content counterparts.[17] According to one research study, half of all clicks on mobile ads are accidental.[18]

Omni-channel

There is a growing realization among even those brands that remain satisfied with digital advertising that the ability to buy, target and optimize banners is now 'table stakes', as Yext Chief Marketing Officer

(CMO) Jeffrey Rohrs explains, in an 'increasingly complex landscape'. This complexity of multiple channels – with complementary content needs – raises challenges for brands as they transition from a paid, push-media mindset to creating a thriving content ecosystem. Retailers and CPG brands are expanding content outwards from phones and desktop computers and into in-store kiosks and other retail experiences.

Intel has partnered with Turner and Mark Burnett to produce a reality show spawning a cosmos of content, online and offline.[19] 'A consumer seeing 10 sequential pieces of content is more valuable to us than seeing the same banner ad 10 times', said Becky Brown, Intel's vice president of global marketing and communications, and director, Digital Marketing and Media Group.

Marriott's David Beebe also shared (at a recent conference) that the company has repurposed content that resonates on its owned digital media channels for out-of-home billboard executions, quipping, 'a multi-tiered paid model for digital content is as juicy an opportunity as a brand could hope for'.

With customers consuming more digital content than ever, expectations shift with each brand experience. They quickly realize which companies deliver content at the right time, when they need it most, and which brands continue to push the square peg of advertising into the round hole of new technology experiences. Consumers expect contextual relevance in messaging that is based on their existing relationship with the company, their purchase history and the mode of communication – which is increasingly mobile in nature.

In order to deliver an effective content mix, companies must become intimately aware of every stage of the digital customer journey, for multiple personas (if not complete personalization). 'Who, What, Where, When and Why' are critical factors for consideration, from awareness through advocacy, as attention is scarce and fragile through every step. This trend towards hyper-personalized content during 'micro-moments' of the brand experience is spurring a retreat from programmatic advertising that automates the experience, as consumers grow sceptical of brands that simply pretend to know their needs based on browsing data.

Figure 1.5 Output versus engagement with branded marketing content by month, 2015

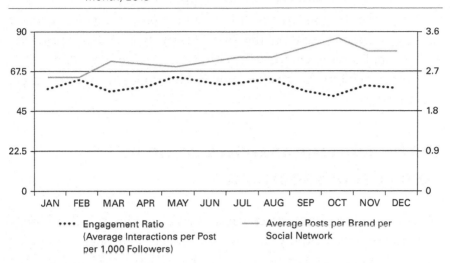

•••• Engagement Ratio
(Average Interactions per Post
per 1,000 Followers)

——— Average Posts per Brand per
Social Network

SOURCE TrackMaven http://trackmaven.com/resources/content-marketing-paradox-revisited/

As screens and devices proliferate, together with growth of in-store beacons and near-field sensors, marketers are beginning to lean heavily on real-time messaging in owned and earned channels. The ability to swiftly respond to events and triggers is critical to capitalizing on sporadic consumer behaviours. Visa's Shiv Singh, SVP of marketing, leads efforts to be more 'in the moment' with consumers, explaining that 'real-time messaging is about to be the primary interface for everything we do'.

More screen use on the go also increases the difficulty of targeting consumers as they channel-hop to purchase. No longer does one message, meant for one paid medium, suffice. Marketers are discovering that a robust content strategy is critical, one that addresses the different behaviours, needs and expectations at every step of the digital decision journey. Successful strategies rely heavily on multiple data sources and address different demographics, personas, and geosegments, with different journeys mapped for every relevant platform and channel.

As mobile traffic is expected to multiply tenfold by 2019,[20] these trends will only accelerate as the need for small-screen content outweighs the pressure of securing traditional advertising budgets. Companies are expected to gravitate towards mobile and social content marketing in the coming years, as their high effectiveness and low cost prove to increase consumer trust and improve the customer experience.

Brands that respond to this shift by simply producing more content are likely to miss out on the opportunity that content provides. For example, research from TrackMaven (Figure 1.5) shows that increased social media posting is inversely proportionate to engagement rates.[21]

Better content analytics combat advertising's foothold

Measuring advertising's effectiveness is an age-old puzzle that has yet to be fully resolved. Many advertisers claim click-through rates prove effectiveness of digital banners, while other diehards stick to 'increased brand awareness' as their mode of measurement. The analytical grey area of advertising is pushing marketers towards content, as they can more easily measure their yields in multiple channels using methods that tie directly to business results.

Content metrics can be intricately examined at each phase of the customer journey, assuming the correct technologies are in place to track customer behaviours (ie CRM, loyalty programmes, social sign-ins, app profiles, etc). Curata provides a model for categorizing the plethora of content metrics available, grouping them into two categories: performance and operations metrics. Example performance metrics are centred on consumption, retention, sharing, engagement, marketing pipeline impact and sales pipeline impact, while operations metrics are tied directly to production and cost.[22] Including measurement as part of an overarching 'content journey' strategy is necessary to prove results and justify investments.

Promises of brand awareness or nebulous engagement metrics no longer cut it when fighting for company resources. As one source, who prefers to remain anonymous, elaborates: 'A lot of CMOs earned their seat at the table because of their contributions to brand awareness, but when they started talking about other metrics, everything got superfluous.' The interviewee continues: 'CEOs are demanding more, requiring other data-driven metrics that can directly correlate activities and align human and capital resources to business objectives. Knowing the data side means more job security.'

Recommendation: build a customer-centric marketing strategy

Shifting the media mix away from advertising and into content marketing requires just as much cultural change as it does resource reallocation. We recommend marketers follow three key recommendations to refocus their company around more engaging content that satisfies customer needs and business goals:

- Create a foundational content strategy before pursuing specific tactics.
- Invest across the customer journey, realigning the marketing mix accordingly.
- Build the right team with the right resources at its disposal.

Create a foundational content strategy before pursuing specific tactics

Although 70 per cent of B2B marketers are producing more content this year than last, a corresponding amount of organizations are doing so without a documented content strategy in place first.[23] This results in inefficiencies and missed opportunities, as well as an inability to measure success due to a lack of concrete goals. For B2C marketers, lacking a documented strategy also means being significantly less likely to be successful.[24]

Investing in content marketing requires an investment in a content strategy that outlines plans for the development and management of content. It should encompass persona development, content creation, repeatability, delivery, governance and the ability to achieve business goals by maximizing the impact of content. Focus on outcomes, not volume, and how to get there operationally and organizationally. Lacking a documented strategy means being significantly less likely to be successful.

A solid content strategy foundation also sets the stage for the adaptation of appropriate technologies and platforms. When a content strategy is tied directly to overarching company and departmental goals and processes, brands are able to respond more efficiently to new media that may emerge. 'Future proof' your content strategy today in order to be prepared for the inevitable content marketing needs of the internet of things, wearables, beacons, sensors and even smaller mobile devices.

Invest across the customer journey, realigning the marketing mix accordingly

Although traditional marketers may be more familiar with focusing advertising tactics on the top of the funnel, content marketing thrives when it is applied differently to every phase of the entire digital customer journey. Content marketers push to create an engaging brand experience during all phases of decision making, purchase and post-purchase support.

Successful customer retention and advocacy strategies are dependent on customizable (ideally, personalized) content that continues to serve consumers and build favourable brand reputation long after any purchase is made.

Rather than strategizing around channel targeting, focus on the behaviours and the needs your customers have during each phase of their journey. Advertising focuses on where you can push your message for the greatest impact, whereas content marketing considers how the message will be consumed, by whom, when, under what circumstances and to what end. Content marketing asks, 'When will the message deliver the most value?'

Make marketing commitments according to customer connection goals in order to add that ultimate value. To do this, marketers must construct detailed content plans that map out how modular content can be repurposed across owned, earned and paid channels, depending on where a customer turns in his or her time of need. These plans should sync with internal editorial calendars and process workflows to ensure efficient resource allocation.

Build the right team with the right resources at its disposal

Leaders looking to beef up their organizational content engine should examine the skill sets of the employees and third-party partners (agencies and vendors) in their marketing arsenal. It is likely that existing teammates were hired for skill sets that skew towards traditional advertising and media needs, with some marketing crossover, or for a very specific channel-oriented purpose (social media management, for example). Similarly, large agencies typically have evolved to offer digital, social or mobile services over time, with strong roots in advertising and PR.

Conversely, experienced professionals who stand out and contribute to a well-oiled content machine include journalists, bloggers and – most recently spawned – the content 'storyteller'. Storytellers are well versed in understanding both brand messaging goals of the traditional marketer and how best to convey them to customers, depending on their lifestyle and purchase data. If existing employees and partners don't have these skills, leaders should consider offering a continuing education programme or hiring from the outside to fill the gaps.

Once the ideal team is built, it needs to be equipped with the tools to succeed, too. Aim to integrate any existing measurement tools wherever possible, focusing on those that measure specific return on investment (ROI) metrics and allow for efficient customer data analysis and action.

Notes

1 EMarketer (2014) [accessed 6 January 2017] Consumers Get Engaged With Rich Media, *Emarketer* [Online] http://www.emarketer.com/Article/Consumers-Engaged-with-Rich-Media/1011282

2 Fingas, R (2015) [accessed 6 January 2017] Apple's Safari Claims 55% of US Mobile Browser Usage, 10.5% Desktop Share, *Appleinsider* [Online] http://appleinsider.com/articles/15/04/22/apples-safari-claims-55-of-us-mobile-browser-usage-105-desktop-share

3 Slefo, G (2015) [accessed 6 January 2017] Report: For Every $3 Spent on Digital Ads, Fraud Takes $1, *Advertising Age* [Online] http://adage.com/article/digital/ad-fraud-eating-digital-advertising-revenue/301017/

4 Sullivan, L (2013) [accessed 6 January 2017] Banner Blindness: 60% Can't Remember the Last Display Ad They Saw, *MediaPost* [Online] http://www.mediapost.com/publications/article/196071/banner-blindness-60-cant-remember-the-last-disp.html

5 Guppta, K (2015) [accessed 6 January 2017] 3 Ways YouTube Pre-Roll is Forcing Marketers to Rethink Video Advertising, *Contently* [Online] https://contently.com/strategist/2015/03/12/3-ways-youtube-pre-roll-is-forcing-marketers-to-rethink-video-advertising/

6 Adweek (2014) [accessed 6 January 2017] Nearly 25% of Video Ad Views are Fraudulent and 6 Other Alarming Stats, *Adweek* [Online] http://www.adweek.com/news/technology/7-things-you-need-know-about-bots-are-threatening-ad-industry-161849

7 Adform (2017) [accessed 6 January 2017] [Online] http://site.adform.com/resources/collateral/whitepapers

8 Bruell, A (2015) ANA Hires Investigative Firms to Prove Agency Rebate Allegations, *Advertising Age* [Online] http://adage.com/article/agencies/ana-taps-firms-investigate-rebate-allegations/300803/

9 Kantrowitz, A (2014) [accessed 7 January 2017] Kraft Says it Rejects 75% to 85% of Digital Ad Impressions Due to Quality Concerns, *Advertising Age* [Online] http://adage.com/article/datadriven-marketing/kraft-rejects-75-85-impressions-due-quality-issues/295635/

10 The CMO Club (2015) [accessed 6 January 2017] Marketing is a (Buyer) Journey, not a Destination – a CMO Solution Guide via the CMO Club in Partnership with IBM [Online] http://thecmoclub.com/news-item/marketing-is-a-buyer-journey-not-a-destination-a-cmo-solution-guide-via-the-cmo-club-in-partnership-with-ibm/

11 Content Marketing Institute (2016) [accessed 6 January 2017] B2B Content Marketing: 2016 Benchmarks, Budgets and Trends – North America, *Content Marketing Institute* [Online] http://contentmarketinginstitute.com/wp-content/uploads/2015/10/2016_B2C_Research_Final.pdf

12 Yarow, J (2015) [accessed 7 January 2017] GE CMO: I'm Done Advertising on Prime-Time TV, *Business Insider UK* [Online] http://www.businessinsider.com/ge-cmo-im-done-advertising-on-prime-time-tv-2015-12

13 TechCrunch [accessed 14 February 2017] [Online] https://techcrunch. com/2012/10/24/online-ad-survey-most-u-s-consumers-annoyed-by-online-ads-prefer-tv-ads-to-online-want-social-media-dislike-button-and-reckon-most-marketing-is-a-bunch-of-b-s/

14 TrustE Privacy Index (2015) [accessed 14 February 2017] Internet of Things Edition [Online] www.truste.com

15 Neff, K (2015) [accessed 6 January 2017] Unilever Finds Social Media Buzz Really Does Drive Sales, *Advertising Age* [Online] http://adage. com/article/digital/unilever-social-media-buzz-drive-sales/300426/

16 Perez, S (2014) [accessed 6 January 2017] Majority of Digital Media Consumption Now Takes Place in Mobile Apps, *TechCrunch* [Online] http://techcrunch.com/2014/08/21/majority-of-digital-media-consumption-now-takes-place-in-mobile-apps/

17 Chen, B (2015) [accessed 6 January 2017] Putting Mobile Ad Blockers to the Test, *The New York Times* [Online] http://www.nytimes.com/ 2015/10/01/technology/personaltech/ad-blockers-mobile-iphone-browsers.html

18 Felix, S (2012) [accessed 6 January 2017] Mobile Advertising's Darkest Secret: Here's the REAL Error Rate for 'Fat Finger' Clicks, *Business Insider* [Online] http://www.businessinsider.com/ error-rate-for-mobile-ad-fat-finger-clicks-2012-10

19 O'Connell, M (2015) [accessed 6 January 2017] Mark Burnett, Turner and Intel Partner for Reality Competition 'America's Greatest Makers', *The Hollywood Reporter* [Online] http://www.hollywoodreporter.com/live-feed/mark-burnett-turner-intel-partner-816036

20 Cisco (2016) [accessed 6 January 2017] Cisco Visual Networking Index: Global Mobile Data Traffic Forecast Update 2015–2020 Whitepaper Document ID:1454457600805266 [Online] http://www.cisco.com/c/en/us/solutions/collateral/service-provider/ visual-networking-index-vni/white_paper_c11-520862.html

21 TrackMaven (2017) [accessed 6 January 2017] The Content Marketing Paradox Revisited, *TrackMaven* [Online] http:// trackmaven.com/resources/content-marketing-paradox-revisited

22 Deshpande, P (2016) [accessed 6 January 2017] The Comprehensive Guide to Content Marketing Analytics and Metrics, *Content Marketing Forum* [Online] http://www.curata.com/blog/the-comprehensive-guide-to-content-marketing-analytics-metrics/

23 Pulizzi, J (2014) [accessed 6 January 2017] New B2B Content Marketing Research: Focus on Documenting your Strategy, *Content Marketing Institute* [Online] http://contentmarketinginstitute.com/2014/10/2015-b2b-content-marketing-research/

24 Content Marketing Institute (2016) [accessed 6 January 2017] B2C Content Marketing: 2016 Benchmarks, Budgets and Trends – North America, *Content Marketing Institute* [Online] http://contentmarketinginstitute.com/wp-content/uploads/2015/10/2016_B2C_Research_Final.pdf

Content marketing versus content strategy

02

As more and more marketers consider how content can work for them to rebalance the digital marketing, advertising and media mix, a certain degree of confusion is beginning to obfuscate discussions and debates. Two very distinct disciplines, content strategy and content marketing, are beginning to blur. And if they are not blurring, too many people carelessly use the terms interchangeably.

It is clear that content marketing and content strategy are not interchangeable concepts, nor do they refer to the same thing. There is, though, a huge degree of interdependence.

Let's begin with their foundational definitions for consideration:[1]

Content strategy: the planning, development and management of informational content. Content strategy must encompass content creation, repeatability, delivery, governance and ability to achieve business goals by maximizing the impact of content.

Content marketing: the creation and sharing of content for marketing purposes. In digital channels, content marketing refers to content that resides on properties the brand owns or largely controls from a content perspective (website, social media, syndication).

I like Ahava Leibtag's take on the issue.[2] The head of Aha Media Group says content strategies are about repeatable frameworks, and content marketing is about building relationships.

Content strategy is what makes content marketing effective, yet according to multiple sources, including my own research, some

75 per cent of organizations are operating content marketing initiatives without a foundational strategy.[3]

Content strategy is the foundation of content marketing

Back in the Web 1.0 era of the 1990s, content strategy (although no one called it that) was primarily relegated to the user experience and website development processes. Your own website was pretty much the only thing online you could control or influence, content-wise. Content strategy has since blown beyond the walled garden and expanded to embrace auditing, analysing, creating, disseminating and governing content in a myriad of channels. From more dynamic websites to the entire scope of Web 2.0 options out there in the wild, companies must now consider how those same rules and processes apply to the entire mix – offline included.

Today, content strategies are robust and focus on repeatable frameworks. They are not something marketers create, but rather implement. Content strategy underpins the implementation of content marketing tactics. Without examining the competitive landscape, current assets, gaps, resources, the market, and plenty of other aspects of a content strategy, content marketing barely has a leg to stand on. Content strategy is the foundation, a structure, an analysis of resources and needs, and a system in place to measure results. If you don't have that strategy in place, all you are doing is Facebooking, or blogging, or tweeting with no real purpose or overarching goals.

'Content strategy plans for the creation, publication and governance of useful, usable content.... The content strategist must work to define not only which content will be published, but why we are publishing it in the first place. Otherwise, content strategy isn't strategy at all: it's just a glorified production line for content that no one really needs or wants.'

Kristina Halvorson, founder and president of Brain Traffic, a web content agency

Breaking down the content strategy formula

Creating a content strategy can be a complex process with many moving parts. Luckily, we can help you to break down the *how* and *why* behind content strategy, beginning with assessing your current situation and initial steps to get moving in the right direction.

To answer the quintessential 'where are we now?' wayfinding query, begin with conducting a content audit. Content audits assess your current content and determine how to make it work best with search engine optimization (SEO) principles. As you are sifting through content archives in every digital channel, you will ask yourself questions such as:

- What content can be used as-is, without changes?
- What content needs to be tweaked to continue using or use in a different channel?
- What content is unusable and needs to be thrown out or otherwise archived?
- What content supports both our user and business goals?
- What media are optimal (eg text, images, video, mobile, etc)?
- Who owns, produces, designs, distributes and publishes this content?

As part of your content discovery process, also conduct internal interviews with all relevant content stakeholders. Use these interviews to uncover existing content workflow and approval processes (within departments and interdepartmentally), identify content owners for each channel, and assess what content goes where and why.

Use the table template in Table 2.1 to track the findings of your content audit.

Audits uncover needs, gaps, weaknesses and inconsistencies you would otherwise never find. They reveal much-needed gaps in process, style, maintenance and other aspects of content governance and process. Moreover, stopping at that one baseline audit is not an option. It is the benchmark from which future audits will be conducted.

Please, don't skimp. Audit, at the very least, twice per year.

Table 2.1 Content audit template example

Page/Sub-Section	Page Name	Type of Content	Source of Content	Owner/Approver/Publisher	What's It About?	Support User/Business Goals?	Findable and Used? Analytics	Clean, Professional, Logically Organized?	Keyword/Metadata/SEO
1.1	Home	xxxxxx	xxxxxxx	xxxxxx	xxxxxx	xxxxxx	xxxxxx	xxxxxx	xxxxxx
1.2	Widget Page	xxxxxxx	xxxxxxx	xxxxxx	xxxxxx	xxxxxx	xxxxxx	xxxxxx	xxxxxx
1.3	About Acme Corp	xxxxxx	xxxxxx	xxxxxx	xxxxxx	xxxxxx	xxxxxx	xxxxxx	xxxxxx

10 steps to building a content strategy

After you have completed a thorough content audit, you can move on to the nuts and bolts of creating a comprehensive content strategy. Use the insights you uncovered in the audit to inform the strategic pillars below. Get this part right, and you will be ready to run a newsroom (or, at least, a well-oiled content machine)! The strategic pillars are:

1 page tables;

2 editorial calendar;

3 style guide;

4 personas;

5 keyword list;

6 brand brief;

7 editing guidelines;

8 graphics and/or digital asset repository;

9 submission brief;

10 maintenance plan.

STEP 1 page tables help define content requirements

Page tables, also known as content outlines, are useful for defining content requirements for your web pages, social channels and other media, prior to creating content. By creating page tables, you can separate the content and content objectives from the style. This allows your organization to approve the subject matter and messages without people getting distracted by things like style and tone.

To make that clear: you prepare the page table so that everyone can agree the content before anyone even thinks about writing copy. Your copywriters then have an easier task, because any feedback will be about their style and tone, not about content. See a sample page table in Figure 2.1.

Figure 2.1   Page table template example

Content title:	*Use a clear, descriptive title that simply explains what is on this page. The title may be specified in the information architecture (IA) document. Try to be descriptive rather than funny or punny*
Template type:	*Which type of content page is this? Does it need to fit into a predefined page template? Have you seen the wireframes for this templates?*
Business area:	*Is this content owned, managed or represented by a specific area of the business?*
Stakeholders:	*• Which people are responsible for approving this content?* *• Which people can sign it off or request amendments?* *• (name names!)*
Expiry date:	*When will this content expire? How regularly should it be checked for accuracy and relevancy?*
Audience:	*Who is this content aimed at? What type of people will be reading it?*
Objectives:	*• What is this content designed to achieve?*
Key messages:	*• What brand messages do we need to convey here?*
Services and products:	*• Which services or products is this page selling?*
Calls to action:	*• Where should readers be directed?* *• What is the goal for readers?*
Authors:	*Who writes and edits the content for this page?*
Resources:	*Where can writers find the information they need to write this page?*

SOURCE Kristina Halvorson (2009) *Content Strategy for the Web*, New Riders, Berkeley

STEP 2 an editorial calendar establishes content creation

An editorial calendar establishes what content will be created when, in what format and for which content channel. A digital editorial calendar also tracks the connections for that content, including how the content will be repurposed and amplified in social media channels.

The editorial calendar (see template in Figure 2.2[4]) should address the questions:

- How much content?
- How often is the content published?

Figure 2.2 Sample content editorial calendar

Editorial Calendar for Weekly Post Frequency

Publish Date	Status	Post Topic	Post Title	Slug url	Keyword Research	Goal	How will you promote it	M T
	AUTO-COLOUR OPTIONS: Just type: Scheduled, Ready to Proof, Draft, Idea, or Not Started	AUTO-COLOUR SERIES OPTIONS: Select cells and click 'Format > Conditional Formatting'				[Example: newsletter signups, event registrations, downloads, shares, visits etc]	[Example: newsletter, social media, Pinterest campaign, blog partnership, blogger outreach, some combo of above etc]	
31/12/2014	Scheduled	January Home Cure	Join the January Home Cure	home-cure	apartment therapy, home cure			
7/1/2015	Scheduled	painting single walls	Partial Paint Jobs: 5 Ways to P	paint-one-	Paint one wall, how to paint one wall			
14/1/2015	Ready to Proof	cool prints (new year)	Purposeful Prints: 10 Visual Re	purposeful	quote prints, purposeful prints			Starts
21/1/2015	Draft	mindfulness	10 Mindful Minutes: Get a Fres	how-to-be-	how to add mindfulness			
28/1/2015	2nd Draft	small space garden How To	How to Grow 100 Pounds of P	how-to-grow	how to grow potatoes			
4/2/2015	Idea	How to Make Frozen Soap But	How to Make Frozen Soap But	make-frozen	how to make frozen soap bubbles			
11/2/2015	Idea	Before/After: Beige	Before and After: From Beige to	beige-to-be	beige to colour			ojects:
18/2/2015	Scheduled	Kids and Housework	Ideas for Getting Kids Involved	kids-house	how to get kids to help, kids housework, kid			
25/2/2015	Draft	How To Kitchen Colour	5 Ways to Add Colour to Your K	add-kitchen	add colour kitchen, kitchen colour			
4/3/2015	Not Started	Rental Kitchens	7 Ways to Rescue a Rental Kitchen					
11/3/2015	Not Started							
18/3/2015	Not Started							as a P
25/3/2015	Not Started							
1/4/2015	Not Started							
8/4/2015	Not Started							
15/4/2015	Draft		Tips for Creating a Mindful Home					+ Bat
22/4/2015	Not Started							
29/4/2015	Not Started							
6/5/2015	Not Started							
13/5/2015	Idea	Colourful Kitchen	A Bright Happy Vintage Kitchen					

SOURCE Goodshows.org

- When, specifically, will the content publish? And, how does it fit into an overarching content schedule?
- What are the content requirements?
- What keywords will each piece of content focus on?
- Where will the content publish?
- Who is responsible for every step of the content, from creation to publication?

STEP 3 create style guides for both writing and design

Style guides are documents that outline the rules and guidelines for the creation of branded content artefacts (see the Nokia sample style guide on the left-hand side of Figure 2.3[5]). We recommend you create style guides for both written pieces and those visually designed.

Writing style guidelines should include rules for grammar, usage, style, tone and voice. Note if the guidelines vary based on channel (eg social versus mobile versus website). Written style guides are often based on standard sources, such as an Associated Press style guide.

Design style guidelines are the visual counterpart to the writing style guide. They should include rules around the treatment of photos, images, embedded videos, fonts, colour schemes, attribution and text–image relationships. Again, consider any differences in visuals from one medium to the next.

STEP 4 identify, research and target archetypal personas

Personas are fictional characters, based on customer data, who represent various segments of your target audience(s). They help content stakeholders to understand whom you are producing content for, which, in turn, helps your team to select topics, define key themes and tailor your message according to relevant customer interests.

Data sources to leverage in persona creation include:

- website analytics;
- market research;

Figure 2.3 Sample style guide (Nokia) and rules that design style guidelines should cover

Nokia N9 speaks human

The tone and language we use is straightforward and conversational. This means no overly technical words, obscure acronyms and industry jargon.

When writing copy for your app, always ensure it's as friendly and natural as possible; read your copy out loud.

Note that you can also localize your apps.

Don't Use: *'Unable to open Gallery'*
Use: *'The Gallery won't open'*

Don't Use: *'Verify settings'*
Use: *'Now check your settings'*

Don't Use: *'Synchronize your calendar with the device'*
Use: *'Sync your calendar'*

Design style guidelines are the visual counterpart to the writing style guide.

They should include rules around the treatment of:

- photos;
- images;
- embedded videos;
- fonts;
- colour schemes;
- attribution;
- text-image relationships;
- and consider any differences in visuals from one medium to the next.

SOURCE Nokia [Online] http://harmattan-dev.nokia.com/docs/ux/pages/Tone_and_Language.html

- social conversations;
- conversion data;
- demographic data.

Each persona created will have different behavioural patterns, preferences, predilections, social traits, hangouts and more. See Figure 2.4 for a sample persona.

Based on customer research, a shipping container company created multiple personas and mapped where each constituency spends their time online (see Figure 2.5). Each line of business within the corporation conducts its own research to assess hot platforms for its unique target audience(s).[6]

Another impressive example of putting content personas into action comes from Procter & Gamble (P&G). The CPG company chose to target the typical buyer of its thousands of household products – mothers – during its official sponsorship of the 2012 Olympic Games. This strategic decision was made in lieu of competing for access to key athletes, and P&G has continued to renew its 'Thank You, Mom' campaign for every Olympics since its initial 2012 run. Its most recent ad for the 2016 Rio Games has already garnered 13.9 million views on YouTube.

According to a company statement about its 'Thank you, Mom' 2012 Olympics content campaign: 'While P&G may not be in the business of athletic equipment, sports drinks or athletic apparel, we

Figure 2.4   Sample content persona

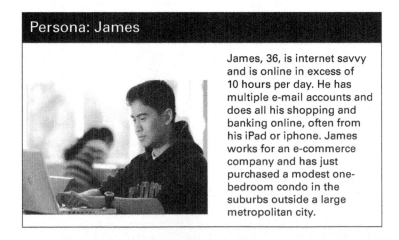

Figure 2.5 Sample customer persona map

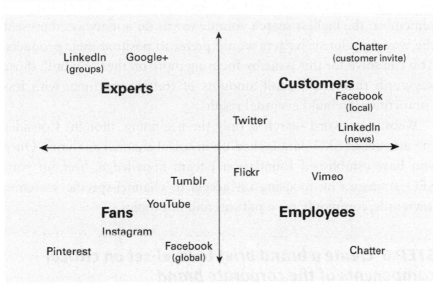

are in the business of helping Mom. We will be using our voice in the London 2012 Olympic Games to acknowledge Mom's rightful place in the 2012 Games.'[7]

The results of focusing on Mom? P&G has estimated that its 'Thank You, Mom' campaign for the 2012 summer Olympics in London resulted in a $500 million sales lift.[8] It was the most successful campaign in P&G's 175-year history, increasing brand portfolio familiarity by 22 per cent, favourability by 13 per cent and trust by 10 per cent. Brand recall of ads was also 38 per cent higher than other US Olympic Sponsors.[9]

STEP 5 generate a keyword list based on SEO research

Based on search engine optimization (SEO) research, a keyword list is a list of words and phrases most critical to your business, products and services when it comes to being found online. If you do not have an SEO expert on staff, anyone and everyone involved in content creation should receive foundational training in SEO and how to appropriately use keywords (and other SEO principles) in content creation.

Free SEO services such as Google AdWords' Keyword Tool can aid in generating a robust and comprehensive keyword list. But remember: the highest search volume words do not always represent the way the content writers would prefer to position their products. You can solve for this issue by focusing more on the 'long tail', those keywords that draw small amounts of traffic over time, with less competition, to build eventual results.

Website keyword search is only the beginning, though! Consider the amount of SEO data locked up in social channel analytics. Once you have established foundational team knowledge, beef up your SEO strategies by focusing on access to channel-specific searches, keywords, commonly used phrases and hot topics.

STEP 6 create a brand brief to level-set on critical components of the corporate brand

Corporate brand briefs are one-page-long descriptions of the corporate brand that all content strategists can reference to ensure continuity. Brand briefs typically include thoughtful narrative that encompasses:

- brand values;
- brand mission;
- key products and services;
- brand impact;
- target customers;
- brand 'personality'.

Liken an internal brand brief to the 'About Us' page on a corporate website, except with the inclusion of more private, employees-only information about what the brand stands for and how it typically conveys its positioning in the media.

STEP 7 thorough editing guidelines ensure high-quality content

Editing guidelines are a checklist that editors (and in many cases, copy editors) use to ensure only high-quality content is published in brand channels. Editing guidelines must complement existing writing and graphic style guides.

It is the editor's job to uphold all the style guide requirements. They are also responsible for checking facts, ascertaining that submitted content is original, validating hyperlinks, proofing images to ensure they are properly labelled and tagged, and a variety of other critical housekeeping tasks. We will review staffing for content marketing further in Chapter 5.

STEP 8 a graphics and/or digital asset repository speeds production efficiency

Have a collection of ready-to-use and commonly used images such as logos, executive portraits and product shots that the content team can easily find and deploy. Many software solutions exist to assist with the storage and classification of such assets (more on technologies in Chapter 9), though your company's intranet or server may be able to do the job in the interim. Depending on needs, you may also want to make multimedia material available in this manner.

STEP 9 submission briefs help with freelancer management

A submission brief is a written (and sometimes visual) outline of expectations and concepts for outside content contributors. Submission briefs help speed up the editing and production process, as they align contractors on all content style guidelines.

STEP 10 remove, recycle and archive content according to a maintenance plan

Not all content is created equally as sustainable with changing trends, themes and messaging strategies. A content maintenance plan outlines guidelines for when to assess content for its removal, recycling (reusing on other channels) and archiving (for potential future updating and use). The maintenance plan should address the entire content life cycle.

Content marketing connects strategy with customers

If not today, then soon, your marketing spend will shift away from advertising and direct response campaigns and into content initiatives that strengthen ties and deepen relationships with customers and prospects. The best way to prepare is to start developing content marketing initiatives. In the previous section, you have completed your homework by researching and developing a solid content strategy framework around these content marketing efforts. Now, on to marketing implementation.

As a reminder, content marketing differs from content strategy in that it is the creation of actual content for marketing purposes. In digital channels, it refers to content that resides on properties the brand owns (eg website) or largely controls from a content perspective (social media channels, or syndication). It is earned and owned media (which we will discuss more in Chapter 3), implemented in long-term initiatives rather than short-term campaigns. In turn, it forces the evolution of your marketing team from advertisers to storytellers in order to reach customers.

> 'Content marketing is a marketing technique of creating and distributing relevant and valuable content to attract, acquire and engage a clearly defined and understood target audience – with the objective of driving profitable customer action.'
>
> *Joe Pulizzi, Content Marketing Institute*

The three types of content marketing

Although storytelling is an important component of some forms of content marketing, it is not synonymous with every implementation. There are three types of content marketing and, as a general rule, only one of them classically 'tells a story'. The other two content marketing modes are equally important, and often follow the rules of a story arc, while not adhering to other rules of narrative. Here are the three types of content marketing:

1 *Content that entertains*. This is the most likely of the three types of content marketing to 'tell a story'. Think viral video, comic strip or webisode. Whole Foods' Do Something Reel film series[10] is a prime example, and so was 2016's viral hit from Squatty Potty, 'This Unicorn Changed the Way I Poop'[11] (see Figure 2.6). Chipotle's 'The Scarecrow'[12] is another standout in the genre, prompting every agency with a fast-food account to receive a 'build me one of these' phone call. *The Lego Movie* (2014) is truly an advanced level of entertaining content marketing, and also an example of the highest level of content maturity I have indentified in my research: monetizable marketing, with a $550 million box-office take. Entertaining, storytelling content need not always be video, there are certainly other forms. But increasingly, storytelling is going visual and audiovisual, given that those formats are easiest to consume on the small screen and are more frequently shared in social channels.

2 *Content that informs and/or educates*. This type of content informs prospects to help them evaluate options, products or services, and make decisions. It is overwhelmingly the choice of B2B companies, as well as B2C products and services with a high need for information/education or longer consideration and sales cycles. Informative/educating content can also, post-purchase, enhance the customer experience and lead to cross-selling or upselling.

Figure 2.6   Squatty Potty's viral entertaining content marketing hit, 'This Unicorn Changed the Way I Poop'

SOURCE Squatty Potty (2016) [Online] https://www.youtube.com/watch?v=YbYWhdLO43Q

Marketing software maker Hubspot, for example, publishes enormous volumes of extraordinarily useful content for digital marketers and advertisers, rivalling that of trade publications in the space. American Express's OPEN Forum has been a content-marketing poster child for years, but is not a storyteller. Instead, the brand publishes information helpful to small business owners and entrepreneurs (see Figure 2.7).

Figure 2.7 American Express OPEN Forum produces content for small business owners

MANAGING MONEY

A Business Built on Confidence: Women Entrepreneurs Share Their Success Stories

Hear how women business owners from this year's WeFestival event learned to pitch investors boldly and empower their teams.

Maria Pedone

OPEN VOICE

PLANNING FOR GROWTH

The Falcon Lab: How a Print Shop Pivoted by Listening to Its Customers

Just as Borzou Azabdaftari was finalizing the purchase of his printing business, the economy tanked. But by listening to his customer, he was able to pivot and expand into a...

Darren Dahl

BUILDING YOUR TEAM

Is Your Business Stuck in a Rut? Here Are 3 Ways to Help You Get Out

Battling your way through a business rut? If you ∗∗ and your company ∗∗ are in need of a change, these tips can help.

BUILDING YOUR TEAM

Hiring Process: How to Screen Job Applicants

Using screening tools such as job applications. pre-interviews and tests as part of the hiring process may help prevent you from hiring the wrong person.

SOURCE American Express OPEN Forum [Online] https://www.americanexpress.com/us/small-business/openforum/explore/

3 *Utility content.* Utility content helps users to accomplish tasks; think of a mortgage calculator from a bank, a calorie counter from a health or fitness product or service, or estate agent tools that help homebuyers to find properties and assess neighbourhoods. Unsurprisingly, utility content tends to be embodied in apps, and is ideal for mobile content plays. The purpose of utility content is to help nudge a buyer towards a decision, as does the example table from Crutchfield (see Figure 2.8) to calculate how big a flat-screen TV to buy, based on room size.

Which of these three types of content should you invest in? The answer, I'm afraid, is 'it depends'. That is why your content strategy is so essential. You may be able to accomplish your goals with storytelling, or you may require other types of content in addition to, or instead of, storytelling. Without strategy though, it is impossible to tell.

Figure 2.8   Utility table to help buyers choose correct TV size

Screen size	Viewing distance range for 1080p HDTVs	Screen size	Viewing distance range for 4k HDTVs
40"	5.0–8.3 feet	40"	3.3–5.0 feet
43"	5.4–9 feet	43"	3.6–5.4 feet
50"	6.3–10.4 feet	50"	4.2–6.3 feet
55"	6.9–11.5 feet	55"	4.6–6.9 feet
60"	7.5–12.5 feet	60"	5.0–7.5 feet
65"	8.1–13.5 feet	65"	5.4–8.1 feet
70"	8.75–14.6 feet	70"	5.8–8.75 feet
75"	9.4–15.6 feet	75"	6.3–9.4 feet
80"	10.0–16.7 feet	80"	6.7–10.0 feet
85"	10.6–17.7 feet	85"	7.1–10.6 feet

For HDTVs, we suggest a viewing distance between 1-1/2 and 2-1/2 times the screen diagonal.	To see the extra detail of 4K TVs, you should sit closer — we suggest from 1 to1-1/2 times the screen diagonal.

SOURCE Crutchfield [Online] http://www.crutchfield.com/S-oNhcHCFWH16/learn/learningcenter/home/TV_placement.html

It is high time brands stopped doing content for content's sake. Planning, benchmarking and attaching content initiatives to a strategy are necessary steps to take for content marketing to work effectively and efficiently. Always begin with strategy, and communicate the difference between the two terms to stakeholders early and often. Refine both strategy and execution on an ongoing basis, based on priorities, goals, learnings and measurement (more on metrics in Chapter 10).

Finding the right content mix: Coca-Cola's 70/20/10 plan

Coca-Cola, a mature content marketer, has perfected its mix of content marketing types over the years. The beverage giant uses a framework called the '70/20/10 content plan'[13] (see Figure 2.9) to ensure they offer the content their audiences want, while also leaving room for innovation.

In summary the 70/20/10 content plan is divided into three parts:

- 70: they plan on 70 per cent of their content to be low risk. By this they mean content that has consistently worked well and achieved results in the past. It doesn't mean boring and definitely doesn't mean low quality.

- 20: 20 per cent of the content that they produce will spin off from what has worked in the past. It basically means a more detailed, in-depth and quality version of the content created for the 70 per cent.

- 10: the final 10 per cent of content will be extremely high risk. These completely new ideas and concepts will often end up being one of two things: something that worked tremendously well or something that failed terrifically.

The lesson learned from Coca-Cola is to be creative and experiment with new ideas. Why? Because that 10 per cent that is high-risk today may turn into just the type of content consumers want 70 per cent of the time in the future.

Figure 2.9 Coca-Cola's 70/20/10 content plan, visualized

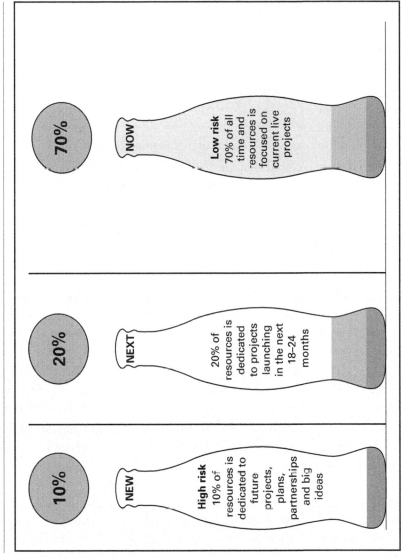

SOURCE Adapted from https://www.linkedin.com/pulse/2014102914565C-9245190-how-jid-coke-become-the-world-s-largest-social-brand (Jeremy Waite, October 2014)

Notes

1 Lieb, R (2016) [accessed 6 January 2017] Content Strategy Workshop (Contently Executive Summit: Finance), *Slideshare* [Online] http://www.slideshare.net/lieblink/content-strategy-workshop-for-contently-finance-summit

2 Leibtag, A (2016) [accessed 14 February 2016] Online It All Matters [Online] http://ahamediagroup.com/

3 Lieb, R (2016) [accessed 6 January 2017] Rebecca Lieb's Blog [Online] http://rebeccalieb.com/blog/rebecca-lieb

4 Find and Convert (2016) [accessed 6 January 2017] Editorial Calendar, Find and Convert [Online] http://www.findandconvert.com/wp-content/uploads/2011/11/editorial-calendar-sample.png

5 Nokia (2016) [accessed 6 January 2017] Tone and Language, Nokia [Online] http://harmattan-dev.nokia.com/docs/ux/pages/Tone_and_Language.html

6 Sprung, R (2012) [accessed 6 January 2017] 7 Companies that Totally 'Get' Their Buyer Personas, Hubspot [Online] http://blog.hubspot.com/blog/tabid/6307/bid/33749/7-Companies-That-Totally-Get-Their-Buyer-Personas.aspx

7 P&G (2012) [accessed 6 January 2017] P&G Sponsors More Than 150 World Class Athletes at the London 2012 Olympic Games, *P&G* [Online] http://news.pg.com/press-release/pg-corporate-announcements/pg-sponsors-more-150-world-class-athletes-london-2012-olymp

8 Weir, K (2014) [accessed 6 January 2017] Olympics-Sponsor P&G Sets More Modest Target for Winter Games, *Reuters* [Online] http://www.reuters.com/article/olympics-pg-sponsor-idUSL6N0KC13K20140106

9 Chiat, J (2013) [accessed 6 January 2017] P&L Proud Sponsor, *AEF* [Online] http://www.aef.com/pdf/jay_chiat/2013/p&g_olympic_proudsponsor.pdf

10 Whole Foods (2012) [accessed 6 January 2017] Whole Foods Market® Do Something Reel Film Festival Goes Online, *Whole Foods* [Online] http://media.wholefoodsmarket.com/news/whole-foods-market-do-something-reel-film-festival-goes-online

11 Squatty Potty (2015) [accessed 6 January 2017] This Unicorn Changed the Way I Poop #squattypotty [Online] https://www.youtube.com/watch?v=YbYWhdLO43Q

12 Chipotle Mexican Grill (2013) [accessed 6 January 2017] The Scarecrow [Online] https://www.youtube.com/watch?v=lUtnas5ScSE

13 Blinman, D (2012) [accessed 6 January 2017] What Coca-Cola Can Teach Us About Content Marketing, *Social Media Today* [Online] http://www.socialmediatoday.com/content/what-coca-cola-can-teach-us-about-content-marketing; Simone, S (2012) [accessed 6 January 2017] 3 Content Marketing Ideas You Should Steal From Coca-Cola, *Copyblogger* [Online] http://www.copyblogger.com/coca-cola-content-marketing/; Pulizzi, J (2012) [accessed 6 January 2017] Coca-Cola Bets the Farm on Content Marketing: Content 2020, *Content Marketing Institute* [Online] http://contentmarketinginstitute.com/2012/01/coca-cola-content-marketing-20-20/

Converged media

03

As a marketer, you are likely quite familiar with three distinct media channels: paid, owned and earned:

- 'Paid media' is advertising. It summons images of banner ads, search engine marketing ads, TV spots or billboards.

- 'Owned media' is comprised of corporate assets such as the company website, a blog or a YouTube channel (primarily your own content marketing efforts).

- 'Earned media' is participatory, it is asking for comments, feedback or other forms of social and/or media amplification. It is characterized by online and offline word of mouth, reviews, forums, media coverage of PR efforts and social media updates. Media can be earned anywhere that people discuss products or brands.

These distinct media are beginning to converge. Soon, they will be inextricably entwined. Gone are the days when marketers could spoon-feed pre-fab sales pitches to apathetic consumers. Welcome to the empowered buyer: a savvy and dynamic customer who continually flits among channels, devices and media types. This consumer is armed with and continually seeking out new information, with multiple options of devices of screens to supply that information, all backed up by an ever-expanding network of peers and references.

Advertising, or 'paid' media has traditionally led marketing initiatives, both online and off, but advertising no longer works as effectively as it did unless bolstered by additional marketing channels. Owned and earned media are vital to campaigns, helping to amplify and spread brand messages across a myriad of complex paths that consumers follow across devices, screens and media. Investment in all three media types increased in 2015, signalling continued brand commitment to reaching consumers with connected media messaging (see Figure 3.1).[1]

Figure 3.1   Media investment split among paid, earned and owned media

| Paid media | % increasing budget | 61% |
| | % of budget allocated | 39% |

| Owned media | % increasing budget | 67% |
| | % of budget allocated | 35% |

| Earned media | % increasing budget | 71% |
| | % of budget allocated | 26% |

SOURCE Oracle (2015) [Online] https://blogs.oracle.com/marketingcloud/new-2015-marketing-budget-benchmarks

Marketers who fail to reconcile paid, owned and earned media today will be at a distinct disadvantage in the future when, in less than 10 years, most media will encompass elements of paid, earned and owned. To arrive at this state, brands must change the way marketing departments are organized, build new models to effectively collaborate with agency and vendor partners, shift budgets, and realign metrics and key performance indicators (KPIs) to effectively measure and assess both creative and media initiatives.

Defining converged media terminology

With the cultural and technological shifts we see in marketing today comes the need to identify, define and standardize terms to streamline discussions in our diverse set of ecosystem connections (see Figure 3.2).

In order to discuss the interplay of paid, earned and owned media, let's first define each of these terms as they apply to digital channels (see Figure 3.3):

- *Paid media* encompasses any form of display or broadcast advertising. In digital channels, paid media includes banner ads, pay-per-click (PPC) search ads, advertorials, sponsorships, sponsored links and pay-per-post blogging. The common factor of all these channels is that they are a form of advertising for which a media buy is necessary. In 2015, 13 per cent of brand digital spend went towards PPC, while 6 per cent was invested in display advertising.[2]

Figure 3.2 The convergence of paid, owned and earned media

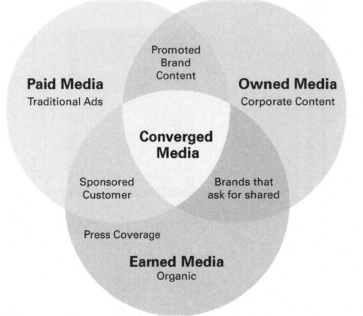

SOURCE 'The converged media imperative: how brands must combine paid, owned, and earned media', Rebecca Lieb and Jeremiah Owyang, Altimeter Group (2012) [Online] http://rebeccalieb.com/sites/default/files/downloads/120719%20Converged%20Media%20RL-JO.pdf

- *Owned media* are all content assets that a brand either owns or largely controls. Owned media channels include websites, microsites, branded blogs, videos and the brand's own(ed) presence on social media and social network channels such as Facebook, Twitter, YouTube, Flickr, etc. Owned media is largely content marketing, ie, content a brand owns and/or publishes that involves no media buy. Owned media received 10 per cent of digital marketing spend among brands in 2015.[3]

- *Earned media* is user-generated content created and/or shared by users. Types of earned media include consumers' social media posts, tweets, reviews, videos, photos and open online communities. Another component of earned media is mentions in media or on social channels that are the result of PR or media relations. For brands, earned media is the most elusive and difficult of the three channels; while it can be influenced, it cannot be directly controlled.

Figure 3.3 Converged media example source: the gap on Twitter and Facebook

Example: What does paid/owned/earned look like on Facebook?

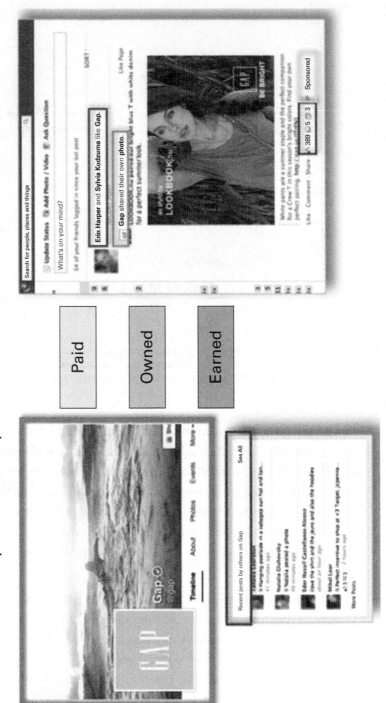

Outlying channels do not neatly conform to the categories of paid/owned/earned media. This is to be expected from some forms of digital media. Online contests and sweepstakes, for example, are often hybrids of paid, owned and earned media. And as mentioned above, shared media ('likes', 'retweets', 'shares', etc) are considered by some to be a wholly separate channel from earned media. Moreover, shared media may or may not contain original content (eg a comment or other earned media) added by the sharer. Co-created content is another category that could be assigned to earned or shared media. We acknowledge these arguments, but for the purpose of this book we will consider 'shared' media to be part of earned.

Converged media utilizes two or more channels of paid, earned and owned media (see Figure 3.4). It is characterized by a consistent storyline, look and feel. All channels work in concert, enabling brands to reach customers exactly where, how and when they want, regardless of channel, medium or device, online or offline. With the customer journey between devices, channels and media becoming increasingly complex, and new forms of technology only making it more so, this strategy of paid/owned/earned confluence makes marketers impervious to the disruption caused by emerging technologies.

Through the emergence of the digital web, social channels, cloud-based technologies, mobile platforms – and shifting notions of

Figure 3.4   Converged media example: earned + paid

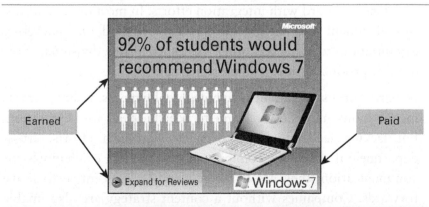

Bazaarvoice deploys paid advertisements with user ratings and reviews. Microsoft advertises with transparency; shoppers click on the ads to learn more from their peers.

SOURCE Bazaarvoice (2012) [Online] http://www.bazaarvoice.com/

convenience – consumers are dancing a new dance in the way they make purchasing decisions. Brands today are challenged to intercept these elusive customers and cut through the media clutter, regardless of whatever channel consumers are engaged with. Converged media is happening; if marketers do not take action, marketing effectiveness will suffer.

Brands lag in deploying a converged media experience

Internally, brands are organized in marketing sub-groups that are territorial, competitive and political. They compete amongst themselves for budget, as well as prominence. The following patterns emerge:

- Mindset varies by department; social team often catalyses change. Brands are only very slowly becoming aware of the need to integrate paid, owned and earned media due to fragmentation of teams within the company. This realization is usually sparked in that part of the organization tasked with social media management, already deploying social ads on Facebook or Twitter. These marketers see the need for paid/owned/earned integration but they lack the authority, budget and clout to get their peers in other marketing divisions on board with integration efforts. In most organizations, this alignment and integration stretches beyond the marketing organization to embrace other customer-facing divisions, most notably product groups and customer service.

- Departmental silos hinder converged deployments. Other marketing divisions may slowly begin to see the need for integration, but lacking leadership that oversees all media efforts, cross-departmental authority, common success metrics or channels for communication, they are hampered and lack incentive to move forwards. Companies without a content strategy are also unable to progress in this environment, as they lack the content marketing assets to maintain presence in owned channels, as well as to effectively and rapidly respond to earned media. Brands cannot sit back and wait for an external partner to take the lead on integration. It is up to them to organize effectively and align external vendors and agencies. This will only happen if they are proactive and instigate change internally, as well as externally.

- Disparate tools leave marketers kneecapped at the workbench. Brands struggle with a panoply of software spanning content management systems (CMSs), marketing automation, advertising management, analytics, dozens of social tools and multiple customer relationship management (CRM) systems. They are forced into integrating disparate systems, which handicaps their ability to use these tools to provide a consistent customer experience. Integrated digital marketing suites are emerging, but a schism between adopting best of breed versus one-size-fits-all will persist.

Brands cannot deploy converged media alone, however. They must coordinate agency partners to reach the dynamic customer. This includes:

- Avoiding a campaign-focused mindset in favour of sustained engagement. Traditional digital advertising agencies tend to be focused on channels where they have historical expertise. Often, these rollouts are short term, based on campaign or advertising flights, yet often with clear measurable results. On the flip side, long-term engagement social agencies span multiple quarters on one effort, but struggle to measure business ROI.

- Uncovering opportunities by lessening myopic channel focus. Agencies are often specialized and do not feel their counterparts in other focus areas are competent in integration. Digital agencies claim that social agencies lack larger brand perspective, while social agencies say that media buyers ignore long-term engagement. In any case, by not integrating, agencies are missing opportunities.

- Helping agencies to keep up through their frustrations with ever-changing tool sets. Most agencies are struggling to move into new channels outside of their core expertise. Social agencies are deploying social ads within social networks but are often disconnected from larger media buying initiatives. On the flip side, digital agencies have deployed social capabilities but are often limited to shorter-term campaigns. To solve this, we expect mergers and acquisitions between the various constituents to provide a cohesive converged media solution. Finally, these service providers must constantly invest in research to keep track of the changing tool set of brand monitoring, Facebook campaign software, social media management tools, content management systems, and more.

Converged media: 11 success criteria

While all ecosystem players possess at least some pieces of the converged media puzzle, no one constituency holds all the pieces in one place. There is, however, a set of baseline needs that brands and their ecosystem partners must have in order to succeed with converged media. We view this new paradigm of creative development as analogous to a chemistry lab in which marketers must conduct and monitor numerous experiments involving many moving parts in order to concoct successful formulae (see Figure 3.5).

A Strategy

1 *Understand the changing forces of converged media*: when it comes to implementing an integrated paid, earned, owned strategy, brand marketers must possess an understanding of the changing forces of converged media, including emerging practices, content types, technologies, channels, behavioural and other trends. Strategists typically build this awareness by conducting an audit to first understand where the brand sits relative to these forces (content, technology, industry, consumer behaviour, channels, etc).

'Look around to see what paid, owned and earned trends look like today, in digital, in your industry, for your consumers; then do an internal audit', advises Gary Stein, former executive VP of strategy for iCrossing. While there is no one-size-fits-all in the successful integration of paid, earned and owned media, success is contingent upon understanding what will resonate within the paradigm (internally and externally) of your organization.

Figure 3.5 Converged media lab – top success criteria

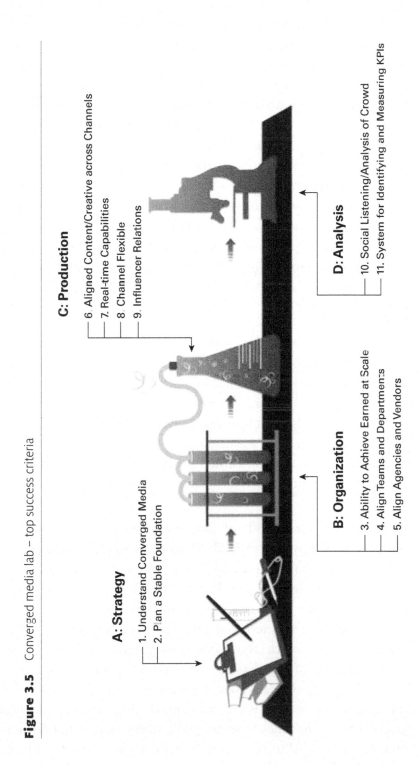

A: Strategy

1. Understand Converged Media
2. Plan a Stable Foundation

B: Organization

3. Ability to Achieve Earned at Scale
4. Align Teams and Departments
5. Align Agencies and Vendors

C: Production

6. Aligned Content/Creative across Channels
7. Real-time Capabilities
8. Channel Flexible
9. Influencer Relations

D: Analysis

10. Social Listening/Analysis of Crowd
11. System for Identifying and Measuring KPIs

2 *Plan a stable foundation*: many marketing and communications departments are executing on one, two or even three media channels, yet these are disparate executions with little insight or relationship to one another. We continually hear tales of overlapping budgets, varying (sometimes conflicting) objectives between teams, and siloed or redundant communications internally and externally between agencies or vendors. The insights that come with analysing earned media instruct and inform the areas in which to amplify using paid and where to innovate with respect to owned. Owned media provides the platform upon which earned and paid can exist and is foundational to the brand presence and messaging, which inspires earned. Paid media helps drive volume to owned and earned channels, and ultimately what amplifies the brand message.

B Organization

3 *Ability to achieve earned at scale*: while earned media is the most challenging to measure for direct ROI, it is also the most powerful medium for achieving brand goals such as advocacy, loyalty, retention and, ultimately, increased sales. But quality earned alone is not enough; brands must leverage paid and owned media to drive quantity. Many brands, agencies and vendors reiterate that the main challenge to scale in earned media (and for the industry at large) lies in the immaturity of the technology and how it impacts agility.

Michael Chin, former VP of marketing and business development for SocialFlow, explained: '[Growing earned] comes down to comparing what your customers are saying about the brand with what the wider social audience is talking about in their own conversations. It's that data-driven portion that allows you to adjust in real time, but accessing it has been a difficult nut to crack for the industry – we're largely driven on gut intuition today. Scale and maturation of this has to involve a data-driven approach.' Achieving earned at scale does not happen overnight; rather it is an ongoing effort of consistent brand messaging, reaching the right people at the right times from the right angles, supported through listening and publishing tools, media agency partners and a fundamentally agile approach.

4 *Align teams and departments*: the most simultaneously challenging, yet essential, element to streamlining converged media execution is overcoming the cultural silos that exist internal to the organization. Brands emphasize alignment in a number of historically autonomous areas: ownership, communication/collaboration, campaign goal(s) and budget. In the past, communication between the ad-buying team and customer service, communications/PR and social strategists, and influencer relations and the creative team (to name a few combinations) is limited. Paid, earned and owned stakeholders must meet at the table to plan initiatives, content, creative, media and strategies that link them. Without partial ownership, there is a risk of channels becoming weak links and afterthoughts rather than essential components of the larger initiative and strategy.

5 *Align agencies and vendors*: as stated earlier in this chapter, the importance of alignment extends beyond the internal organizational structure, externally, to agencies and vendor partners. Brands' partner companies require briefs that define the scope of paid, owned and earned convergence. Each will have individual areas of specialization and expertise, yet full-picture visibility is essential for all partner companies.

C *Production*

6 *Aligned content/creative across channels*: humans build relationships with brands in the same ways that they do with other humans: through ongoing interactions, establishing trust and mutual benefit/value. As digital channels continue to evolve, so do the audience's options for consumption. Aligning content across channels is paramount for driving consistent brand messaging, value, look and feel. Stakeholders across paid and owned channels must also be aligned on branding elements from day one.

7 *Real-time capabilities*: to be effective in paid, owned and earned media, integration must be agile. Agility is a derivative of effective listening, measurement and resource allocation, as well as market, cultural and media awareness. The organization must also facilitate agility in its converged media strategy by providing the proper

labour resources, buy-in from stakeholders, communication channels between these stakeholders (internal and external) and empowerment to act. Real-time capabilities (measurement, benchmarking, reporting, attribution, engagement, support, etc) are what enable this agility and the ability to respond and act rapidly and efficiently – something particularly critical in earned media. We will discuss real-time content marketing further in Chapter 8.

8 *Channel-flexible*: the empowered and dynamic customer has choices; choices in the platform they use to consume information, how social they want to be in the process, and the time of day they wish to do so. Thus, it is important for brands to extend their presence across multiple channels and platform types. With consistent messaging, brands can reach their audiences wherever they are at any time. This distributed presence is a cornerstone to successful paid, earned and owned integration, both in terms of brand ubiquity from a consumer standpoint and revealing demographic and behavioural insights from the brand standpoint.

9 *Influencer relations*: in a world where 90 per cent of customers' online purchases are influenced by reviews,[4] influencers comprise a key constituent that brands simply cannot afford to ignore. Influencers can play a role to amplify the brand message across all media types, whether touting the product in an unprompted 'earned' setting, being the voice of a 'paid' campaign, or even through offering guidance or advice on an 'owned' platform. Analysts, bloggers, celebrities, expert practitioners and news commentators are just a few of these influential consumers who carry large and engaged fan followings.

D Analysis

10 *Social listening/analysis of crowd*: consumers, not marketers, drive successful marketing. No matter the medium (paid, owned or earned), customers determine success. Successful integration of paid, owned and earned media requires agility, both to shift campaign strategies quickly and experiment with pilot campaigns and idea-testing. Listening, monitoring and measurement are instrumental in substantiating this level of rapid decision making. 'Experimentation is absolutely critical', says

Joshua Backer, president of advertising and SVP operations at Unified. Comprehensive measurement and analysis is challenging. Brands inevitably have different needs, metrics, incumbent technologies and integration requirements, regardless of the relative immaturity of the converged media space.

Listening and tracking consumers' behaviour around each media type is paramount to maximizing the impact of the investment. Analysis of the crowd can instruct strategy, while technologies that track individual behaviour can facilitate better engagement on a customer-by-customer level.

11 *System for identifying and measuring KPIs*: measuring the impact of any investment is important, but in the world of real-time marketing, it is essential. Unified's Joshua Backer adds: 'Measure as much as possible! Go as deep as you can into attribution in order to separate the signal from the noise. Focus on what is driving the highest-quality signal.' And so the system for identifying KPIs must instruct the ongoing measurement itself. KPIs should be established at the onset, but brands must also constantly have their ears to the ground for engaging consumers along each step of the customer journey – from consideration to purchase, to support to loyalty. These metrics are fluid and may shift based on customer segment, platform, campaign assets and goals, even external forces such as cultural events, etc. In a world of converged media, they are the foundation from which investment potential is established, understood, optimized and realized. (For more on measurement, see Chapter 10.)

Savvy brands deploy successful converged media

In our research and analysis of brands, agencies and vendors, we found that certain companies are indeed beginning to converge media successfully and with good results. While many brands are converging two media types, few have effectively integrated all three. Figures 3.6 and 3.7 show two case examples of companies combining two or more media types, both online and offline:

Figure 3.6   Owned + earned media

Owned + Earned: The New York Giants bring
social events to owned venues, generating earned buzz

The New York Giants digital team created a year-round programme of social promotion and curation campaigns in order to cultivate engagement with fans on and off the field. Beginning in the pre-season, the Giants would become the first professional sports team to integrate live tweets both in the stadium and on TV for viewers at home. Using social curation, tweets were enabled on-site via the stadium Jumbotron, while simultaneously televised; there were website polls and pre-game Twitter Q&As. The team also created Twitter-based commerce tie-ins for shop.giants.com.

Results: Increased e-commerce sales via Twitter-driven discounts; Twitter followers grew 122.87% in the 2011 preseason (7/28–9/12). Team jumped from ranking 20th to ranking 3rd for most NFL Twitter followers. Halloween Costume Contest Campaign attracted 7,000 votes, driving amplification and awareness.

(Vendor: Mass Relevance)

SOURCE The New York Giants/Mass Relevance (2011)

Figure 3.7   Paid + owned + earned media

Paid + Owned + Earned: Trifecta amplification: paid to owned to earned

A Fortune 100 technology brand paid social influencers to create engaging and authentic content across a number of their own(ed) media properties. This content aligned with themes related to the brand's products and initiatives. The paid content gained earned amplification as influencers shared content across their social networks. Engagement and links were then driven directly to the brand's owned social properties, including their blog, Facebook, Twitter, Google+, Tumblr, and YouTube channel. A total of 121 pieces of content were produced (text, video, infographics, images, etc) across only 24 influencers.

Results: Over 1.1 million social interactions were generated, an average of 9,314 per piece of content.

(Vendor: Social Chorus)

SOURCE Social Chorus (2012)

Recommendations for marketing leaders

Flowing paid, owned and earned into a single media stream requires a champion at the executive level. A series of changes must occur spanning internal organization, working with agency partners and utilizing software providers. CMOs and their teams must make converged media a reality.

First, brands must prepare internally. The need to change how content flows between different groups within marketing is altered, requiring strong leadership. Marketing leaders should:

- Reinforce the goals and opportunities of converged media. Converged media is a shift in how media are deployed. Elements of social, advertising and corporate content are merged into one, with rapid iterations and in-flight changes balanced by frequent engagement. The cost to the organization will be high, so the leadership team must communicate the benefits, including: a cohesive story told across channels, deeper engagement as the crowds' content is integrated, and reduced costs by aligning all internal and partner teams. Unify around an agreed-upon set of data to measure success. Get everyone using the same metrics and the same dashboard.

- Bridge internal teams. To start, marketing leadership will need to guide internal teams together that span corporate communications, media buyers and social teams in order to communicate and tell one story. To do this, new roles may need to emerge that report to marketing leaders and will run day-to-day operations; early titles around content strategists or digital storyteller are taking shape, often stemming from a background in media, editing or journalism. Breaking down silos is essential. Refer to Chapter 5 for additional guidance around organizing for content.

- Hone media creation capabilities. Owned media is increasing in importance – content is the glue that holds this troika together. It is incumbent on brands to develop content strategies that are sustainable and scalable. Specific skills to develop include creating a unified brand voice, building a foundation of content creation that spans all channels, and developing real-time capabilities across all these channels.

The convergence of paid, earned and owned media is a reality. This commingling of media channels is hardly limited to ad hoc occurrences on social networks. Rather, it has become a business model. As consumers become increasingly mobile, paid/owned/earned convergence will intensify. Rapid journeys across multiple digital devices will increasingly blur the lines until almost all distinction between paid, owned and earned media dissolves.

Companies that do not prepare for this convergence now in digital channels will be at a marked disadvantage, for two reasons:

- Paid, owned, earned integration is already bleeding into more traditional forms of media, beginning with television. As traditional forms of media (broadcast, books, periodicals) become more digital, paid/owned/earned convergence will be pervasive.

- As the connected world or 'internet of things' (IoT) becomes a reality, in the coming years media will be embedded into and around common objects. Products, appliances and tools will contain data. Initially, this information will be paid and owned, but very quickly earned components will develop and commingle with other information.

Preparing for paid/owned/earned integration is therefore not just a demand of present reality, but an inevitable necessity of the future of marketing, advertising and communications.

Notes

1 Cooper, N (2015) [accessed 6 January 2017] New 2015 Marketing Budget Benchmarks, *Oracle Marketing Cloud* [Online] https://blogs. oracle.com/marketingcloud/new-2015-marketing-budget-benchmarks

2 Cooper, N (2015) [accessed 6 January 2017] New 2015 Marketing Budget Benchmarks, *Oracle Marketing Cloud* [Online] https://blogs. oracle.com/marketingcloud/new-2015-marketing-budget-benchmarks

3 Bylykbashi, K (2015) [accessed 6 January 2017] Marketers Set to Ramp Up Budgets for 2015, *Marketing Week* [Online] https://www.marketing-week.com/2015/02/26/marketers-set-to-ramp-up-budgets-for-2015/

4 Gesenhues, A (2013) [accessed 6 January 2017] Survey: 90% of Customers Say Buying Decisions are Influenced by Online Reviews, *Marketing Land* [Online] http://marketingland.com/survey-customers -more-frustrated-by-how-long-it-takes-to-resolve-a-customer-service-issue-than-the-resolution-38756

Native advertising 04

Native advertising is an intersection of paid and owned media, and therefore is a form of converged media. It promises very real benefits both to consumers, in terms of a more elegant and seamless user experience, and to the rest of the digital marketing and publishing ecosystem. Developed and deployed correctly, the result can be more effective and engaging messaging that provides welcome economic benefits – so long as sufficient strategy, learning, coordination and transparency are invested upfront.

I define native advertising as follows:

Native advertising is a form of converged media that combines paid and owned media into a form of commercial messaging that is fully integrated into, and often unique to, a specific delivery platform.

The definition of native advertising clearly overlaps with existing definitions of sponsored, branded or custom content, as well as advertorial.

The integrated form that native advertising takes depends on the media vehicle or platform. For example, on publisher sites, native advertising placements are congruent in look and feel to editorial (see Figure 4.1). On Facebook, this could take the form of sponsored stories or Newsfeed ads, or on Twitter, promoted tweets (see Figure 4.2).

While earned media, such as social sharing, is not an inherent element of native advertising, it is an essential adjacent component to many, if not most, native advertising campaigns. Sharing, liking – and otherwise socially promoting native advertising campaigns – promotes, amplifies and extends reach and awareness.

Figure 4.1   Native advertising example

Note: The articles are clearly sponsored content by Quaker State, Travel Oregon and Scotts, as noted above the images in grey boxes. Native advertising on a publisher site takes the form of the publisher's own content, eg long-form article, listicle, slideshow, etc, while echoing the look, feel and user experience of that site.

SOURCE Satirical news site The Onion (theonion.com)

Why native advertising?

The battle for consumer attention has never been fiercer, or more difficult for marketers. With the increased utilization of browser plug-ins that block ads from loading online, it is estimated that 12 per cent of display ads are never seen by humans,[1] translating into US $18.5 billion in ad-spend waste in 2015 alone.[2] Separate from ad-blocker usage, consumers are subconsciously ignoring digital advertising, with 60 per cent suffering 'banner blindness', effectively unable to recall any online banner ads they are exposed to.[3] Add to these facts that 94 per cent of online video viewers skip pre-roll ads before five seconds has passed,[4] and 25 per cent of the few video ad views are fraudulent,[5] and marketers can no longer ignore the need to shift their marketing spend away from traditional tactics towards more engaging content deployments like native advertising.

The creative component of native advertising is content marketing, ie, messaging intended to attract rather than interrupt consumers. Paid placement for attractive content aims to buck the twin trends of banner blindness and shrinking ad revenues. Results are promising: Facebook News Feed ads are 51 times more likely to generate clicks than an identically targeted display ad on Facebook,[6] and according

Figure 4.2 Native advertising examples

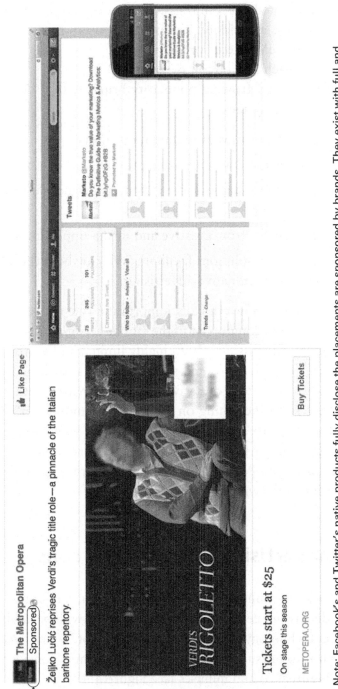

Note: Facebook's and Twitter's native products fully disclose the placements are sponsored by brands. They exist with full and conspicuous transparency and disclosure around the commercial intent of the message.[7]

SOURCE Facebook and Twitter

to Nielsen, a promoted tweet impression drove a 22 per cent average increase in message association compared to users not exposed to promoted tweets.[8] eMarketer predicts that US spending on native advertising will reach $21 billion by 2018.[9]

Native advertising's growing popularity brings with it opportunities for the entire ecosystem:

- For publishers, new forms of premium inventory.
- For social platforms, new advertising products.
- For brands, new opportunities for attention, engagement and message syndication.
- For agencies, benefits from creative and media opportunities.
- For technology, new solutions facilitate and scale both the creative and delivery aspects of native advertising.

It is hard to overstate how critically important a role native advertising serves as a growth component to the mobile ecosystem, where real estate for display advertising is both highly limited and more disruptive to the user experience. Some social networks, such as Twitter, are prepared for the advent of native advertising paired with mobile screens: 'There is no such thing on Twitter as a "mobile ad". Other platforms have had to adapt to the new world, while we haven't. Native is becoming part of that conversation more rapidly because of mobile', shared Jim Prosser, head of corporate, revenue and policy communications for Twitter.

Native advertising: the pros and cons

Like any marketing innovation, native advertising has both advantages and disadvantages. Some of the minuses will be addressed by time and technology innovations – others not. When weighing whether or not to pursue native advertising, one must consider these pluses (see Figure 4.3) and minuses (see Figure 4.4).

In summary, brands and agencies approaching native advertising have the most to gain – but also, the most to be wary of. Publishers, social networks and brands/agencies all stand to benefit from new

Figure 4.3 Native advertising pros

	PUBLISHERS	SOCIAL NETWORKS	BRANDS AND AGENCIES
Users opt-in to content/pull strategy	x	x	x
Combats downward pressure on price/effectiveness of banner ads	x		x
New revenue streams	x	x	x
Life/reach/efficacy of owned media	x		x
Better paid-owned-earned media integration			x
Higher engagement	x		x
Strong potential for mobile platforms	x	x	
Potential for deeper behavioural/contextual data	x	x	x
Reinforce or even improve UX	x	x	
Amplification beyond fans/followers		x	x

SOURCE 'Defining and mapping the native advertising landscape', Rebecca Lieb, Altimeter Group (2013)

Figure 4.4 Native advertising cons

	PUBLISHERS	SOCIAL NETWORKS	BRANDS AND AGENCIES
Scale/labour-intensive	x		x
Lack of landscape clarity, still evolving	x	x	x
Roles are ill-defined	x		x
Metrics/KPIs not fully defined	x		x
Requires strong content ability			x
No 'search juice', per Google	x		x
Content lacks budget/dedicated staff, native included	x		x
Education/training required	x	x	x
Sales team training/pushback (more complex sales cycle)	x		
Consumers may view native advertising as misleading	x		x
Transparency/disclosure issues	x	x	x
Voice, context, environment, authenticity	x	x	x

SOURCE 'Defining and mapping the native advertising landscape', Rebecca Lieb, Altimeter Group (2013)

revenue streams created by native advertising, as well as increased value and relevance to their target audiences because of the opt-in nature of the medium.

At the same time, all players are vulnerable to the infancy of native advertising. This will require education and training, regulations around transparency and disclosure, and a greater emphasis on maintaining the authenticity that consumers expect from the publisher/platform.

Native advertising landscape

As native advertising is unique to its online or in-app placement, there is no one magic bullet product offering. Options differ substantially between three key players – publishers, social media platforms and technology vendors – that serve up solutions for online or in-app placement.

Below is an outline of a sampling of available solutions from all three constituents. Note that the list is by no means comprehensive in scope, but rather representative of key offerings in a new landscape that is rapidly growing, changing and evolving.

Publishers

When it comes to native advertising, we found that publishers do not clearly distinguish it from the more commonly used terms 'sponsored content' or 'promoted content'. In fact, many publishers remark that they have been offering 'native advertising' solutions for brands for five or more years – they just were not using the term.

While the overall concept of native advertising as sponsored content may not be new from the publisher perspective, the accompanying layers of digital complexities do make native advertising a breed apart from yesteryear's standard advertorial. Social platforms offer native advertising opportunities that stray far from what might be considered sponsored content; in fact, they dispense with the publisher altogether. Transparency, disclosure, interactivity, landing pages, social amplification, the sales process, and new wrinkles in maintaining the traditional church/state divide between editorial and publishing are all far from resolved in this emerging, lucrative and, as yet, far-from-established form of advertising.

Figure 4.5   Native advertising criteria on publishing platforms

Native Advertising Criteria: Publishing Platforms

- FULL TRANSPARENCY AND DISCLOSURE OF COMMERCIAL RELATIONSHIP
- MAINTAINS INTEGRITY OF PUBLISHER/EDITORIAL RELATIONSHIP
- ALIGNS WITH PUBLICATION'S STYLE, VOICE, AND POV
- EFFECTIVELY TELLS BRAND STORY THROUGH CONTENT

SOURCE 'Defining and mapping the native advertising landscape', Rebecca Lieb, Altimeter Group (2013)

In most cases, native advertising offerings vary little from one publication to the next. Publishers work directly with brands and their agencies to create content that fits into the following criteria, shown in Figure 4.5.

The native advertising relationship between publishers and brands can be cosy. Publishers offer not only writing services, but also in-house creative to complement articles with imagery, video and accompanying on-page banner advertising to create a total campaign package. It is not uncommon for publishers to find themselves in limbo, playing the familiar roles of editor and journalist while also acting as creative director – often arm-in-arm with the brand's agency partners. According to Mashable CMO Stacy Martinet: 'The best [native] campaigns are collaborative. Our job is to help brands tell their best story without making a sales pitch. We want to drive home their values or differentiators in a way that will really resonate with our audience and spark them to share and explore. The more collaborative we can be with brands and their partners, the better.'

Some publishers, such as Time Inc, have found that native advertising provides opportunities to monetize their vast archives of editorial content. They can resurface, and republish, evergreen content that once appeared on editorial pages in the service of their advertisers.

In addition to requiring clear policies around disclosure and transparency, publishers face the additional burdens of ensuring traditional church/state divisions are not breached by, for example, external media buyers working directly with their editors. Additionally, burdens of training are emerging. Publishers must educate their ad sales teams around native advertising offerings, while highly lucrative sales teams are trained to sell Internet Advertising Bureau (IAB) standard display units, not highly customized solutions. Publishers are only beginning to realize and address this gap.

A few publishers, including Federated Media and Buzzfeed, are establishing formal training programmes for agencies. Purportedly, this is to help them to produce better creative for native formats. Tacitly, it is likely to get native advertising higher on their collective radar.

Publishers offering native solutions continue to grow, varying in publication focus and audience. A recent Online Publishers Association (OPA) survey found that nearly three-quarters say they offer some form of native advertising.[10] Ranging from a one-off sponsored story to a full-fledged article series, transparency is key, and publishers find that maintaining trust with the reader is of utmost importance when deploying native advertising online.

From publishing moguls like Condé Nast and Hearst to digital-age newcomers like Buzzfeed and Mashable, native advertising has crept its way into nearly every arena – B2C *and* B2B publications alike. This has made brand congruence with publication choices more important than ever. If the partnership is not the perfect fit, readers will let the publisher and brand know – in one way or another.

Social media platforms

Native advertising options vary greatly from one social platform to the next, as by their definition they must fit into each platform's unique content delivery specifications and community architecture. For example, looking to Facebook, users will find native ads taking the form of promoted posts – posts within their News Feeds that have been sponsored by a brand. Look to Twitter, and uncover droves of sponsored tweets within your stream that are tailored to your interests that you gave expressed on the platform.

Although the delivery format of native advertising differs from one social platform to the next, by and large social platforms are embracing native advertising as a viable product to offer brands that wish to heighten their customers' experience in a way that is relevant and nonintrusive in comparison to traditional online banner ads. Community building, lead generation and awareness were cited as the most common goals employed with native campaigns on social networks.

In our research, we found that budgets for native advertising campaigns range from several thousand dollars to six-figure deals on Facebook, Twitter and Tumblr, with brands working directly with sales representatives to craft campaigns, write and design creative, execute appropriately and monitor results. Larger campaigns often require a minimum investment, but once brands sign the dotted line, cost per thousand views (CPM) and cost per engagement (CPE) pricing is the norm.

In addition to native advertising product offerings, large social networks are also investing in brand education through onsite workshop sessions, strategy advisement, and sharing real-time best practices during ongoing campaigns. Take Facebook's 'Publishing Garage', for example – a platform that the social network has created to work with mega-agencies and brands to improve how they use Facebook's marketing services to generate results.[11] This type of education helps brands to tell their stories in a way that is not only right for them, but also right for each social network's unique user base.

Technology vendors

We conducted interviews and briefings with many technology vendors providing native advertising solutions, and the resounding chorus heard was increasing scale and relevance.

In the case of native advertising, brands must focus on achieving optimal scale and relevance as a pair, as one cannot survive without the other. Remove scale, and you are left with budgetary issues or short-lived campaigns. Remove relevance, and it is no longer successful *native* advertising. David Fleck, general manager of audience for

Figure 4.6 Foundational equation for native advertising

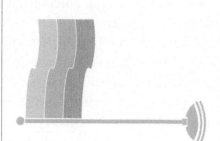

Use a proprietary algorithm to determine what branded content (owned or earned text, images, or video – vendors may work in one content type or all three) receives the most engagement across the web and social platforms.

+

Tag the content with identifiers that can be later used to match it with appropriate audiences, social platforms, and publishers. Disassemble the content package (ie body copy, photos, video) so it can be recombined in new ways in other channels.

=

Constantly optimize native advertising content (often in real or near-real time). The most engaging content can then be used in other digital channels/platforms in native ad units and on social platforms and owned media to create additional experience and amplify ongoing initiatives.

SOURCE 'Defining and mapping the native advertising landscape', Rebecca Lieb, Altimeter Group (2013)

Disqus, noted the importance of scale when considering native advertising programmes: 'We need to enable brands to achieve their goals. Savvy brands with social centres and staffing are proving that they get it, that they need to authentically and directly communicate with their consumer base at scale. With native, you can almost pull that off, but there can still be a scale issue.'

By and large, we found that vendors marry the two by following the equation (Figure 4.6).

Note: Individual vendors do veer from this equation. It is meant to represent the foundations of vendor native advertising solutions as found in our research. Effectively, we see vendors using their unique version of this formula to help brands discover which OWNED media is producing the most EARNED media to populate new forms of PAID media. Native advertising units are simply a bucket or shell for scalable content that can be rotated when the right context arises, and vendors have recognized that.

Recommendations: critical elements for successful native advertising campaigns

For brands considering a native advertising approach, it can seem a daunting task. Confusion around content strategy, internal roles, channel selection, and more, are enough to make any digital strategist's head spin.

We recommend beginning the planning process for incorporating native advertising into your marketing arsenal by fulfilling the eight critical elements for success:

1 *Transparency, disclosure and trust*: as with the early days of search advertising – when paid search results required clear delineation from organic ones, or word-of-mouth marketing and pay-for-play blogging – industry standards have emerged around the disclosure of what is paid and what is editorial content on a variety of media platforms in addition to individual publisher policies. The US Federal Trade Commission (FTC) released a set of guidelines

around native advertising in December 2015[12] – guidelines that 70 per cent of publishers are not fully adhering to today.[13] It is absolutely imperative that all parties err on the side of caution: too much, rather than too little, disclosure. Disclose that the placement is commercial in nature, link to policies that govern such placement, and provide a channel for inquiry.

2 *Content strategy*: without strategic directives and governance documents on voice, tone, brand, messaging and positioning, native advertising can easily veer into alliances that strike all the wrong notes. Put in place a foundational content strategy prior to native advertising (or content marketing) executions. Document governance around voice, tone, brand, edit and copy guidelines. Subject native advertising creative to the approval of the content strategy governing body (more on organizing for content in Chapter 5). Additionally, ensure all content is modular and can be decoupled for use in other contexts, channels and platforms. Consider creating a content warehouse that identifies and classifies tagged content so it can be easily pulled for future needs.

3 *Collaboration*: internal departments, agencies and vendor partners must leverage resources and ensure the brand message or story is not fragmented across social and other platforms. Encourage internal collaboration, and begin fielding a list of departments and roles that need to be involved in the native advertising programme workflow. Loop them in as soon as possible to increase cooperation and coordination. Also incentivize external collaboration – this is the brand's responsibility. Contemplate how the brand's current agency partners, sponsorship partners and other vendors may be involved in the native advertising programming process. Agencies often take the lead in first-time native efforts, or at least serve as seasoned consultants. Finally, ensure teams are agile, able to learn quickly, and apply what they have learned to other campaigns and channels.

4 *Earned component*: native advertising is an example of converged media. It is a combination of paid plus owned media. Factoring in ways to share or otherwise amplify the ad/message can contribute greatly to amplifying the message and/or extending the reach of the campaign.

5 *Content portability*: related to, but distinct from, adding an earned component to native advertising campaigns is working to ensure the content/creative can, wholly or in part, travel to other platforms to amplify messaging and increase awareness. Create native advertising executions that can be socially sharable, and track the content that most resonates in social channels. Maintain libraries of content (in partnership with agencies, if needed) that break down into discrete units of text (eg headlines, teaser copy, body copy), images, infographics, video of varying lengths, etc) that can be deployed quickly in a variety of formats and channels.

6 *Training*: native advertising is relatively new in comparison to its traditional ad counterparts, so ad sales teams, creatives, content creators, analytics teams and others in the continuum are likely unschooled in the what's and how's. Already, companies such as Buzzfeed and Federated Media have implemented training programmes to aid understanding of the tactics and strategies behind native campaigns. In your training efforts, start with content strategy training at the brand level, training sales teams in native advertising offerings and advantages. Then train creative, account management teams, media buyers and others in the ecosystem on native tactics and strategies.

7 *Ability to scale*: at present, scale is the most difficult aspect of native advertising, and the one technology companies are working to address. If 'native' means endemic to the platform, pulling up stakes and moving a campaign from one media property to another is difficult to impossible on social platforms. Targeting and retargeting audience segments are still reserved for programmatic advertising buys. Technology solutions such as OneSpot (www.onespot.com) or inPowered (www.inpwrd.com) attempt to take discrete units of content and create display advertising solutions with them. Note that highly portable vendor solutions do tend to scale and travel, but at the expense of being native in the strictest sense. (More contenders and solutions are discussed in Chapter 9.)

Understand that native advertising campaigns executed with digital publishers and/or social media platforms are usually 'exclusive' and cannot be reduplicated elsewhere. Results must match an increased workload. Also remember that publisher-created content for native executions is often contractually limited to that publisher's platform and cannot be used by the brand as creative elsewhere.

8 *Measurement*: understand that each platform has its own unique user base, formal structure, native behaviours and social actions. For example, a 'share' on Facebook results in content being placed into friends' news feeds, while a 'like' opts into future communications by the brand. A tweet is fleeting, while a Pinterest pin lasts until the owner of the account takes it down. In addition, tracking elements, calls to action and other measurable elements can track the ROI of native advertising campaigns. We will dive deeper into measuring content effectiveness in Chapter 10.

Notes

1 Fingas, R (2015) [accessed 6 January 2017] Apple's Safari Claims 55% of US Mobile Browser Usage, 10.5% Desktop Share, *Apple Insider* [Online] http://appleinsider.com/articles/15/04/22/apples-safari-claims-55-of-us-mobile-browser-usage-105-desktop-share

2 Slefo, G [accessed 6 January 2017] Report: For Every $3 Spent on Digital Ads, Fraud Takes $1, *Advertising Age* [Online] http://adage.com/article/digital/ad-fraud-eating-digital-advertising-revenue/301017/

3 Sullivan, L (2013) [accessed 6 January 2017] Banner Blindness: 60% Can't Remember the Last Display Ad They Saw, *Media post* [Online] http://www.mediapost.com/publications/article/196071/banner-blindness-60-cant-remember-the-last-disp.html

4 Guppta, K (2015) [accessed 6 January 2017] 3 Ways YouTube Pre-Roll is Forcing Marketers to Rethink Video Advertising, *Contently* [Online] https://contently.com/strategist/2015/03/12/3-ways-youtube-pre-roll-is-forcing-marketers-to-rethink-video-advertising/

5 Adweek (2014) [accessed 6 January 2017] Nearly 25% of Video Ad Views are Fraudulent and 6 Other Alarming Stats, *Adweek* [Online] http://www.adweek.com/news/technology/7-things-you-need-know-about-bots-are-threatening-ad-industry-161849

6 Coleman, A (2014) [accessed 6 January 2017] Facebook Ad CTR Study – Newsfeed v Display: from the Wolfgang Lab, *Wolfgang Digital* [Online] http://www.wolfgangdigital.com/blog/facebook-ad-ctr-study-newsfeed-v-display-from-the-wolfgang-lab#sthash.eCkTAjWA.dpuf

7 Frey, C (2015) [accessed 6 January 2017] How To Do Paid Promotion on Twitter the Right Way, *Content Marketing Institute* [Online] http://contentmarketinginstitute.com/2015/04/paid-promotion-twitter/

8 Boston, K (2013) [accessed 6 January 2017] Nielsen Brand Effect for Twitter: How Promoted Tweets Impact Brand Metrics, *Twitter* [Online] https://blog.twitter.com/2013/nielsen-brand-effect-for-twitter-how-promoted-tweets-impact-brand-metrics

9 eMarketer (2015) [accessed 6 January 2017] What's the Must-Have Component of Native Advertising?, *Emarketer* [Online] http://www.emarketer.com/Article/Whats-Must-Have-Component-of-Native-Advertising/1012059

10 Marvin, G (2013) [accessed 6 January 2017] 73% of Online Publishers Offer Native Advertising, Just 10% Still Sitting on the Sidelines, *Marketing Land* [Online] http://marketingland.com/73-of-online-publishers-offer-native-advertising-just-10-still-sitting-on-the-sidelines-emarketer-52506

11 Darwell, B (2012) [accessed 6 January 2017] Facebook Works with Brands on Page Post Strategy During 'Publishing Garage' Process, *SocialTimes* [Online] http://www.adweek.com/socialtimes/facebook-works-with-brands-on-page-post-strategy-during-publishing-garage-process/288178

12 Federal Trade Commission (2017) [accessed 6 January 2017] Native Advertising: A Guide for Businesses, *Federal Trade Commission* [Online] https://www.ftc.gov/tips-advice/business-center/guidance/native-advertising-guide-businesses

13 Adweek (2016) [accessed 6 January 2017] Publishers are Largely Not Following the FTC's Native Ad Guidelines, *Adweek* [Online] http://www.adweek.com/news/technology/publishers-are-largely-not-following-ftcs-native-ad-guidelines-170705

Organizing for content

05

Despite an overwhelming trend towards content marketing and the need to continually feed an ever-increasing portfolio of content channels and formats, most organizations have not yet addressed content on either a strategic or tactical level. This chapter explores scalable organizational models for addressing content needs across the enterprise and makes recommendations for a holistic programme.

The content challenge: feed the beast

Brands have evolved into media companies. Some larger enterprises today publish more content on a daily basis than *Time* magazine did weekly, during its heyday. As content marketing steadily encroaches on the budgets and resources allocated to paid advertising (a trend that has accelerated for years),[1] brands suddenly find themselves in the media business in a very real way.

In addition to content in purely owned media channels, we have discussed how many brands are also challenged to create content for social media, converged media, native advertising, advertorial, paid influencer and sponsorships. Content must also be created for an ever-expanding spectrum of media, screens and devices, ranging from smartphones and tablets to emerging platforms such as augmented reality, Google Glass and devices like smartwatches. Figure 5.1 illustrates the panoply of channels and formats that today's marketers must consider as part of an overarching content strategy.

Figure 5.1 Plotting the content marketing ensemble

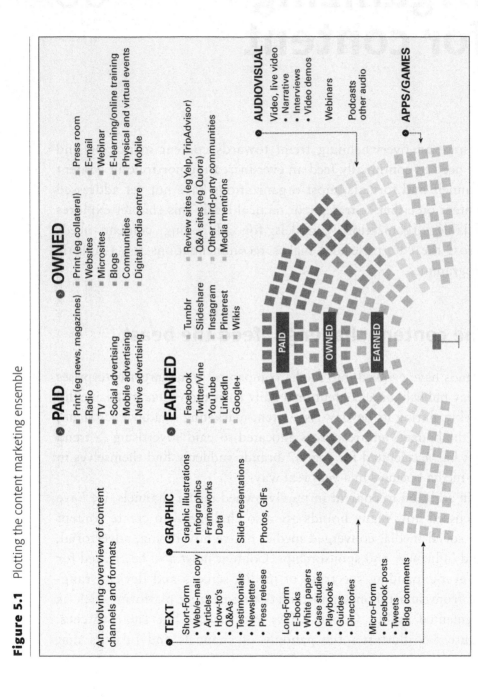

An evolving overview of content channels and formats

● **TEXT**

Short-Form
• Web/e-mail copy
• Articles
• How-to's
• Q&As
• Testimonials
• Newsletter
• Press release

Long-Form
• E-books
• White papers
• Case studies
• Playbooks
• Guides
• Directories

Micro-Form
• Facebook posts
• Tweets
• Blog comments

● **GRAPHIC**
▪ Graphic Illustrations
▪ Infographics
▪ Frameworks
▪ Data
▪ Slide Presentations
▪ Photos, GIFs

● **PAID**
▪ Print (eg news, magazines)
▪ Radio
▪ TV
▪ Social advertising
▪ Mobile advertising
▪ Native advertising

● **EARNED**
▪ Facebook
▪ Twitter/Vine
▪ YouTube
▪ LinkedIn
▪ Google+
▪ Tumblr
▪ Slideshare
▪ Instagram
▪ Pinterest
▪ Wikis

● **OWNED**
▪ Print (eg collateral)
▪ Websites
▪ Microsites
▪ Blogs
▪ Communities
▪ Digital media centre
▪ Review sites (eg Yelp, TripAdvisor)
▪ Q&A sites (eg Quora)
▪ Other third-party communities
▪ Media mentions

● **AUDIOVISUAL**
Video, live video
• Narrative
• Interviews
• Video demos

Webinars

Podcasts
other audio

● **APPS/GAMES**

SOURCE 'Organizing for content', Rebecca Lieb, Altimeter Group (2013) [Online] http://rebeccalieb.com/sites/default/files/downloads/13049%20 Organizing%20for%20Content%20RL.pdf

New channels and platforms, coupled with a trend that de-emphasizes the written word in favour of visual and audiovisual content,[2] creates new skill demands. 'Hire a journalist', a tactic many organizations adopted with the rise of blogging, now is in no way sufficient to address more technical requirements involving higher knowledge of technology, production, design and user experience.

Content responsibility and oversight tends to be both reactive and highly fragmented, as illustrated below in Figure 5.2. This highly typical diagram portrays how one major retail brand divides up content responsibilities between divisions that are not necessarily interconnected or even in regular communication with one another. This fragmented approach leads to inconsistent messaging, huge variations in voice, tone, brand and messaging, and an inconsistent customer experience. The channel divisions themselves tend to be ad hoc, assigned primarily on the basis of hand-raising than any overarching content strategy. Brands find themselves ill-equipped and scrambling to create content that meets both company and user needs. This is no mean feat, particularly with content channel responsibility, ownership and creation dispersed across the enterprise.

Figure 5.2   Where does content live inside the enterprise?

Fragmentation is the Current Norm: How One Major Brand Allocates Content Responsibilities

SOURCE 'Organizing for content', Rebecca Lieb, Altimeter Group (2013)

Organizations must organize for content

Although the overwhelming majority of organizations don't have content divisions in their organizational charts, hiring for content-related roles is on the rise. Since 2011, the number of content marketing job-listings has grown nearly 350 per cent![3] Still, the company divisions where content originates and/or resides (eg customer service, sales and marketing, and communications) remain disconnected and marketing roles have become heavily siloed.

Organizations are not structured to act in concert with regard to content. This lack of orchestration results in duplicative efforts that waste time and money while producing inconsistent messaging. Simultaneous rapid growth in channels and platforms require an ever-greater degree of internal harmony, as well as new skills and strategies around content. As the need to address content, both strategically and functionally, grows exponentially, internal dissonance is coming into tune, albeit slowly.

Like news or entertainment enterprises, companies are challenged to 'feed the beast' on a daily basis. At the enterprise level, a company may have literally hundreds, if not thousands, of websites, product sites and blogs, and dozens of social media channels in which they are active. Large enterprises might boast 5 million e-mail subscribers and multiple millions of unique visitors per month to their websites, even if they are not yet active in social media. Social media only escalates the issues.

Content activities can include touch marketing, communications, social media, community, IT, creative, agency and vendor relationships, customer service, product groups, PR, and possibly dozens of other internal and external stakeholders. Content marketing budgets have been increasing for years.[4] Yet, few organizations have actually made a place for content. Instead, most toss content duties or assignments to already-busy employees who are untrained, ill-prepared, and lack a strategic mandate or incentives to source, create, produce, disseminate, benchmark, measure or manage content.

The demand for content marketing, as well as for the underlying governance of content strategy, has become impossible to ignore. While this need often originally arises on content's front lines – ie communications or social media divisions – content's reach exceeds far beyond these departments to embrace the enterprise as a whole, particularly marketing, advertising, community, CRM, research and development (R&D), IT, knowledge management and PR. What resources are required, internally and externally, to create a foundational content strategy, as well as to execute tactically on production, execution, publication, dissemination and measurement? The C-suite (or board) must understand and recognize that content is needed and is growing in importance. It cannot be an afterthought or something fobbed off on junior, untrained and already-busy employees. Content initiatives must be efficiently organized and financed, efforts cannot be reduplicated across divisions, and strategy should be aligned company-wide.

Organizational content requirements

Orchestrating effective and efficient content requires understanding and planning for the essential elements of content marketing and content strategy. Often, many necessary divisions and skill sets already reside in-house, eg IT and analytics. Yet these operations have little knowledge of, or training in, content goals and requirements. Other requirements, both strategic and tactical, necessitate bringing in new resources. Listed below are the essential elements of content that must be considered by any organization creating content on a regular basis, as well as the organizational models for orchestrating these disparate skills and practices.

Strategy

As discussed in Chapter 2, content strategy is the framework within which content marketing initiatives are executed. It embodies all content-related objectives, processes and governance, from the selection of tools, technologies, staff and partners, as well as the how and what content is produced, to its approval and publishing processes and maintenance. Without a centralized, strategic alignment to why and how content is being produced and the resource allocation for that production, companies too easily fall into the trap of 'we need a blog, or a Facebook page or a microsite'. Efforts are unaligned with goals and appear scattershot.

> 'One thing you want to have is a content strategy so you understand what content you are producing and how it is going to support your overall mission.'
>
> *Alisa Maclin, VP of marketing for IBM's Mobile Enterprise*

Authority/management

To establish both content strategy and ongoing governance and oversight of content initiatives, a content authority is required within the organization. This executive role or governing body must have cross-functional and multi-divisional visibility and purview to efficiently operate, as will be examined in the organizational models described in this chapter's next section (see Figure 5.3).

> 'Content is a team sport. All the content has to work together; all the groups need to work together.'
>
> *Karen Pate, VP of content strategy at iCrossing*

Staff

Many organizations are coming to realize that assigning content duties to untrained and already overburdened staff is not efficient, realistic or capable of creating a scalable solution towards addressing growing content requirements. Marketing organizations active in content marketing say they have roles with 'content' in the title. Those in these roles are either dedicated to or spend a majority of their time on content creation and publication.

Technology

Content requires a plethora of tools for production and measurement, collaboration and management, curation, aggregation, publishing, and more (which we will explore in Chapter 9). Overwhelmingly, we found a disconnect between marketing and IT when it comes to tool selection, capabilities, requirements and cross-functional buy-in. Without content oversight, staff active in content are often expected to work with technology selected by IT. They are end users rather than stakeholders in the selection, implementation and feature set of the content management systems (CMSs), digital asset management (DAM) systems, and other foundational tools. In fact, the bigger and more fundamental the tool, the less input the content staff say they have. This leads to a rogue, workaround culture that inhibits collaboration and sharing. The end result of these workarounds is teams buying consumer-grade solutions, often with duplicative capabilities.

Measurement

'It's all over the board' is a common refrain when marketers are asked if, or how, they measure content. This is partially due to a lack of overarching, cross-divisional strategy, but the multidisciplinary reach of content initiatives creates diverse and often conflicting metrics, ranging from 'engagement' from one group to hard leads or sales for another. This lack of a holistic approach is more apparent in organizations that have no central governing person or body for content. For more in-depth analysis of content metrics, refer to Chapter 10.

Audit

In addition to regularly assessing content effectiveness, quality, quantity, channels, and a host of other criteria, regular content audits also help organizations to track what content assets they own and where they reside. Larger enterprises are increasingly at a loss to know what content exists where in the organization, leading to resource inefficiencies and duplication of efforts.

Unified guidelines and playbooks

Defining what content should and should not be is an essential strategic element. Editorial calendars; workflow maps; editing; style and brand guidelines; rules for voice, tone and brand; and a persona map are foundational for alignment across the groups creating content, both internally and externally.

Training

'We are putting more resources into branded content marketing than into any other area of marketing communications', shared Linda Boff, CMO at General Electric. This holds true in many organizations, yet the majority lack formal content training. There are exceptions. For example, Dell rigorously trains anyone who writes or publishes on behalf of the brand, while Wells Fargo teamed with an industry trade organization to create a content 'university'.

Yet, organizations too often do not have formal training programmes dedicated to content staff. Rather, they hire for specific experience (journalists, and also videographers, designers, etc). Another model is to train outside of marketing, teaching sales, product and customer groups how to recognize stories and write in the brand voice.

Content orchestration: organizational models

To align and enable efficient, coordinated, cost-effective and strategic content strategy, creation and production, companies/brands must organize for content. Band-Aid solutions neither scale nor will work, except in the very short term. Yet, creating a content department, bringing on costly senior talent, is also not always immediately feasible either.

We have identified the following enterprise models (Figure 5.3) for governing the orchestration of content within organizations. The model that any enterprise selects is determined by many factors,

Figure 5.3 How companies organize for content marketing

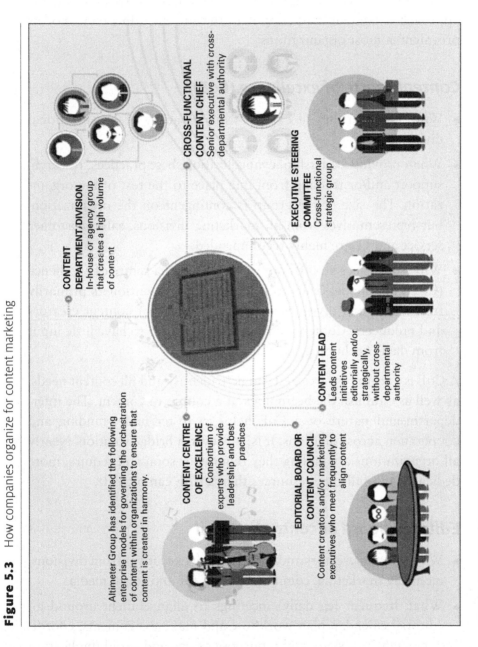

Altimeter Group has identified the following enterprise models for governing the orchestration of content within organizations to ensure that content is created in harmony.

CONTENT DEPARTMENT/DIVISION
In-house or agency group that creates a high volume of content

CROSS-FUNCTIONAL CONTENT CHIEF
Senior executive with cross-departmental authority

EXECUTIVE STEERING COMMITTEE
Cross-functional strategic group

CONTENT CENTRE OF EXCELLENCE
Consortium of experts who provide leadership and best practices

CONTENT LEAD
Leads content initiatives editorially and/or strategically, without cross-departmental authority

EDITORIAL BOARD OR CONTENT COUNCIL
Content creators and/or marketing executives who meet frequently to align content

SOURCE 'Organizing for content', Rebecca Lieb, Altimeter Group (2013)

ranging from budget to the types and volume of content produced, which is why it is important to stress that these models are not hierarchical. Rather, each affords a more systematic, cohesive and strategic approach to content marketing than the current 'adhocracy' models prevalent in most organizations.

Content centre of excellence (CoE)

- Who: a consortium of experts from a variety of organizational divisions.

- What: provide leadership, evangelization, best practices, research, support and/or training from one place to the rest of the organization. The size of the group is contingent on the organization, but representatives from all marketing divisions, sales, customer service and IT are highly recommended.

- Why: sometimes an offshoot of a social media centre of excellence (CoE), this model tends to bring together practitioners primarily from marketing divisions to serve the needs of content creators and producers. Content CoEs are few and tend to have little input from the IT/technology side of the enterprise.

A CoE is a go-to resource and can help identify and fill content needs, as well as establish the beginnings of a culture of content. The interdepartmental nature of a CoE helps to foster understanding and cooperation across divisions. It is, however, a bridge solution. Nearly all organizations are finding they require, or soon will require, more dedicated and full-time resources than a CoE can provide.

Editorial board or content council

- Who: content creators and/or marketing executives from divisions, including marketing, communications, PR and social media.

- What: frequent (eg daily) meetings to align content around an editorial calendar, plan workflow and make assignments, coordinate initiatives, share and repurpose assets, and avoid duplication of efforts. The council examines metrics and analytics on customer discussions and insights to develop the content that should be created based on those insights. A relatively short-term (two months) editorial calendar is built from these findings and decisions are made regarding how content will be adjusted or adapted for regional and/or international dissemination.

- Why: more tactical than strategic. Keeps the trains running.

A board or council keeps content in focus, on the radar, and facilitates communication across departments and divisions, which can lead to real efficiencies and cost savings. But be wary of the fact that, without strategic oversight, an editorial board can get bogged in the weeds of tactics. It can lack executive authority and buy-in, creating the need for the board to spend undue time advocating for themselves across territories and divisions.

Content lead

- Who: an executive who oversees an organization's content initiatives. Titles range from editor-in-chief to global content strategist.
- What: takes a hands-on approach to content creation and execution and works cross-departmentally to coordinate initiatives with stakeholders, IT, vendors and service providers.
- Why: helps prioritize initiatives, gets stakeholders on the same page, and brings strong editorial experience and expertise to the role. This position also goes far in creating underlying strategy documentation such as voice, tone, edit and copy guidelines to unify content initiatives across the enterprise.

A strong editorial background coupled with workflow experience and a knowledge of needs and resources both accelerates and smoothens content-related operations, while at the same time creating and ensuring adherence to a strategic framework. Without cross-departmental authority or significant seniority, though, the content lead is often hampered by departmental barriers (eg working with IT). If lacking a more senior executive champion, the lead can struggle to make known internally both themselves and the resources they offer. Evangelization often becomes an overly burdensome part of the role in larger enterprises.

Executive steering committee

- Who: a cross-functional strategic group comprised of senior executives.
- What: focused on gut checking and approving content from the perspective of product/subject matter expertise, as well as marketing/creative.
- Why: to provide more strategic leadership than an editorial board provides. This unit is contingent on there being an editorial board in the first place.

Strategic oversight and executive buy-in lends to the success of this model. An executive steering committee is well positioned to integrate content with other marketing and advertising initiatives, but can be removed from and/or have little insight into the more tactical, workflow aspects of content.

Cross-functional content chief

- Who: Chief Content Officer, Head of Digital Strategy. The title is not as important as the mandate: a senior executive who is the 'Boss of Content'.
- What: cross-departmental authority, able to set a global content strategy for the organization. May not necessarily have a staff of direct reports, but does possess authority and buy-in from senior management.
- Why: authority, focus, expertise and diplomacy to align the strategic and tactical aspects of content, as well as align initiatives with vendors, agencies and other marketing, advertising and communication streams.

The buck stops with the cross-functional content chief as he or she is, ideally, a benevolent dictator who can align divisions while setting a real strategic agenda. Chiefs have chops in all of content's myriad aspects, from measurement, to technology, to creative. With all their years of experience, though, you can also plan for roadblocks in making the case to the CMO or board of directors as to why they should hire another very senior executive.

Content department/division

- Who: in-house or agency (the latter particularly in the case of multinational initiatives when linguistic and/or cultural differences surround content).

- What: large-scale, high-volume content creation that is often heavily technical, with high demands for mobile, video and higher-quality images. Global capabilities. Strategic and tactical.

- Why: demand exceeds in-house capabilities, both in terms of workflow, talent, skills, technological capabilities and linguistic/cultural/regional/global levels.

This model is the most scalable solution to meet diverse and wide-ranging content needs. However, it comes at a high cost and high commitment. It can be challenging to keep this larger, autonomous group integrated and engaged with non-content marketing initiatives, as a large degree of internal orchestration is also required.

Recognize it's time to organize for content

Organizations with a digital presence, whether their own website or in social media channels, are compelled to produce and publish content, if not on a continual basis then frequently and consistently. This demand will only increase in the months and years to come. Organizations that don't review content needs as such risk a haphazard, inconsistent and unprofessional media presence. A scalable and systematic approach to content strategy and content marketing has become a must-have, not a nice-to-have.

Design strategic foundations, not just production capabilities

In their haste to feed the beast, too many organizations take a short-sighted tactical view towards content orchestration. They implement solutions aimed at systematizing and assigning responsibility for the production queue. Organizing for content is both a strategic and tactical undertaking. Businesses that fail to seriously evaluate how and where content fits strategically and operationally within their organizations will suffer in the short term as they strive to continue to create content without cohesion. They will be at a greater disadvantage in the months and years ahead as content demands accelerate in terms of owned content and converged content hybrids in social media and advertising.

Orchestration and fine-tuning content organizationally is the next, most critical step facing marketing. Follow the recommendations in Figure 5.4 to guide your content organization.

Figure 5.4   Recommendations checklist: make room for content

---

A. Lead with Process

☐ 1. Appoint an empowered cross-functional governor or governing body — a conductor — with executive support and/or authority.

☐ 2. Locate and identify existing content and content sources across the enterprise. Identify where it is being created, housed and how or it is shared.

☐ 3. Identify dotted-line reports (eg internal subject matter experts, customer service, sales).

☐ 4. Create and document efficient production processes, approval systems and schedules.

☐ 5. Create governance documentation (style, edit and brand guides, personas, voice and tone guidelines and editorial calendars that also govern workflow).

☐ 6. Integrate content (owned media) with paid (advertising) and earned (social and PR) media.

☐ 7. Train: Make available and mandatory tiered programmes geared to different stakeholders and managerial levels (creators, producers, managers, senior executives, technology, etc).

☐ 8. Plan beyond 'hire a journalist'. Graphics, video and visual storytelling, as well as multiplatform consideration, are essential to most content strategies.

☐ 9. Hire the right people; bring them in at the right time. Writers, designers and producers require involvement at the beginning of the process, not below the line.

B. Mate with Technology

☐ 10. Be a technology stakeholder, not a mere end user when evaluating, updating, or scoping solutions.

☐ 11. IT integration — an IT partner or member of the IT department should be part of any content board or committee for mutual understanding of requirements.

☐ 12. Involve those stakeholders who will use specific technologies (eg the CMS or digital asset management system) in IT requirement scoping.

C. Follow with Measurement

☐ 13. Define, then align goals, measurement and KPIs.

☐ 14. Share and discuss results across stakeholders.

☐ 15. Constantly evaluate and redefine KPIs and metrics.

☐ 16. Ensure content metrics aren't at odds with stakeholders' individual goals. Example: Collaborators on a single engagement may be comprised of one set of team members who are responsible for customer acquisition, while others strive for engagement.

SOURCE 'Organizing for content', Rebecca Lieb, Altimeter Group (2013)

Notes

1 Vermes, K (2015) [accessed 6 January 2017] Marketers Plan to Shift More Budget to Content Marketing and Native Advertising, *KoMarketing* [Online] http://www.komarketingassociates.com/industry-news/marketers-plan-shift-budget-content-marketing-2017/

2 Mawhinney, J (2017) [accessed 6 January 2017] 42 Visual Content Marketing Statistics You Should Know in 2017, *Hubspot* [Online] http://blog.hubspot.com/marketing/visual-content-marketing-strategy#sm.0001111lnhpu9dflr9a2hhqvuui01

3 Jones, K (2015) [accessed 6 January 2017] 6 New Insights About Content Marketing Hiring Trends and Job Growth, *Marketing Land* [Online] http://marketingland.com/6-new-insights-content-marketing-hiring-trends-job-growth-135821

4 Content Marketing Institute (2016) [accessed 6 January 2017] B2B/B2C Content Marketing: 2016 Benchmarks, Budgets and Trends – North America, *Content Marketing Institute* [Online] http://contentmarketinginstitute.com/wp-content/uploads/2015/09/2016_B2B_Report_Final.pdf and http://contentmarketinginstitute.com/wp-content/uploads/2015/10/2016_B2C_Research_Final.pdf

A culture of content

06

Companies that evangelize, reinforce and institutionalize the importance of content throughout and beyond the marketing organization are more successful in both their marketing initiatives and other success benchmarks such as sales, employee advocacy, customer service, audience engagement, thought leadership and hiring.[1]

When content becomes an ingrained element of an enterprise's culture, the culture functions like a well-oiled engine, producing, circulating and begetting content, creating numerous efficiencies in the process.

Defining a 'culture of content'

A culture of content exists when the importance of content is evangelized enterprise-wide, content is shared and made accessible, creation and creativity are encouraged, and content flows up and downstream, as well as across various divisions. A formalized yet not immutable content strategy is the framework upon which to base culture.

A culture of content is the most realistically achievable level of maturity for the majority of organizations. As content strategy and content marketing continue to gain traction, this chapter examines and illustrates how organizations create and foster a culture for it.

Why a culture of content is emergent now

Content demand

It's not just because brands are publishers that the culture of content is emerging, it's that employees are publishers, too. Some will dismiss this as noise rather than signal, but channel, platform and device proliferation further enables employees to speak on behalf of the brand. Add to that, requests from teams in social media, sales, thought leadership, real-time marketing, recruitment and customer service, and the demand has never been higher for continual content creation, refinement, repurposing and reformatting.

Content is everywhere

Subject matter experts do not solely reside in the marketing department; they come from product, research, senior management and beyond. A customer service representative knows better than the social media team what problems or complaints customers have. Sales staff, whether working on the floor at a retailer or peddling a high-priced, high-tech, long-consideration-cycle product, know what their customers need to learn at various stages of the buying cycle.

Proliferation of media and channels

Not only are demand and need for content growing, so too are the forms that content can take. Content is no longer limited to white papers, blog entries and reports, but is increasingly also video, infographics, billboards, social media posts, GIFs, testimonials, receipts and connected products, among the ever-growing list of new media form factors. The rapid digitalization of culture through channels such as smartphones, social media and connected products and devices is creating an imperative for real-time, dynamic and highly targeted and contextualized content deployment across channels and audiences.

Media convergence

The convergence of paid, owned and earned media also creates a need to efficiently transport and transform content across screens, media and platforms. Content should be part of a well-oiled, well-built, smoothly operating machine. (More about converged media in Chapter 3).

The anatomy of a culture of content

A culture of content resembles an engine in that it streamlines content production and workflows. It also resembles a circulatory system in that it is inherently about sharing, ideation and distributing the value of content across everyone involved.

A strategic, systematized culture of content requires strong leaders with a clear vision to enact and support it. We have identified four primary components of a culture of content, which will be examined in this chapter: inspiration, people, process and content (see Figure 6.1).

Inspiration: the intangibles that fuel a culture of content

Culture in any context is driven by certain intangible but powerful forces. These forces inform, inspire and reinforce the behaviours that define and embody the culture itself, and a culture of content is no exception. Our research identifies three primary forces that fuel a content-centric organizational culture: vision, creativity and risk.

Vision

The idea of a single, shared purpose, mission or goal is paramount to empowering a culture of content because it serves as the baseline of understanding. Establishing a common vision is a critical first step to developing a content strategy and is typically most effective when generated, embodied and exemplified by leadership. Disseminating vision from the top down helps employees to understand how their day-to-day tasks serve a higher purpose and align with organizational and even social or humanitarian objectives.

charity: water, a nonprofit organization that works to provide clean drinking water to developing countries, uses content to drive its vision and its vision to drive content. The vision is to leverage the web's reach to reinvent charity. Because the company is focused on driving individuals to action – that is, to fundraise instead of simply

Figure 6.1 A culture of content is an engine of content

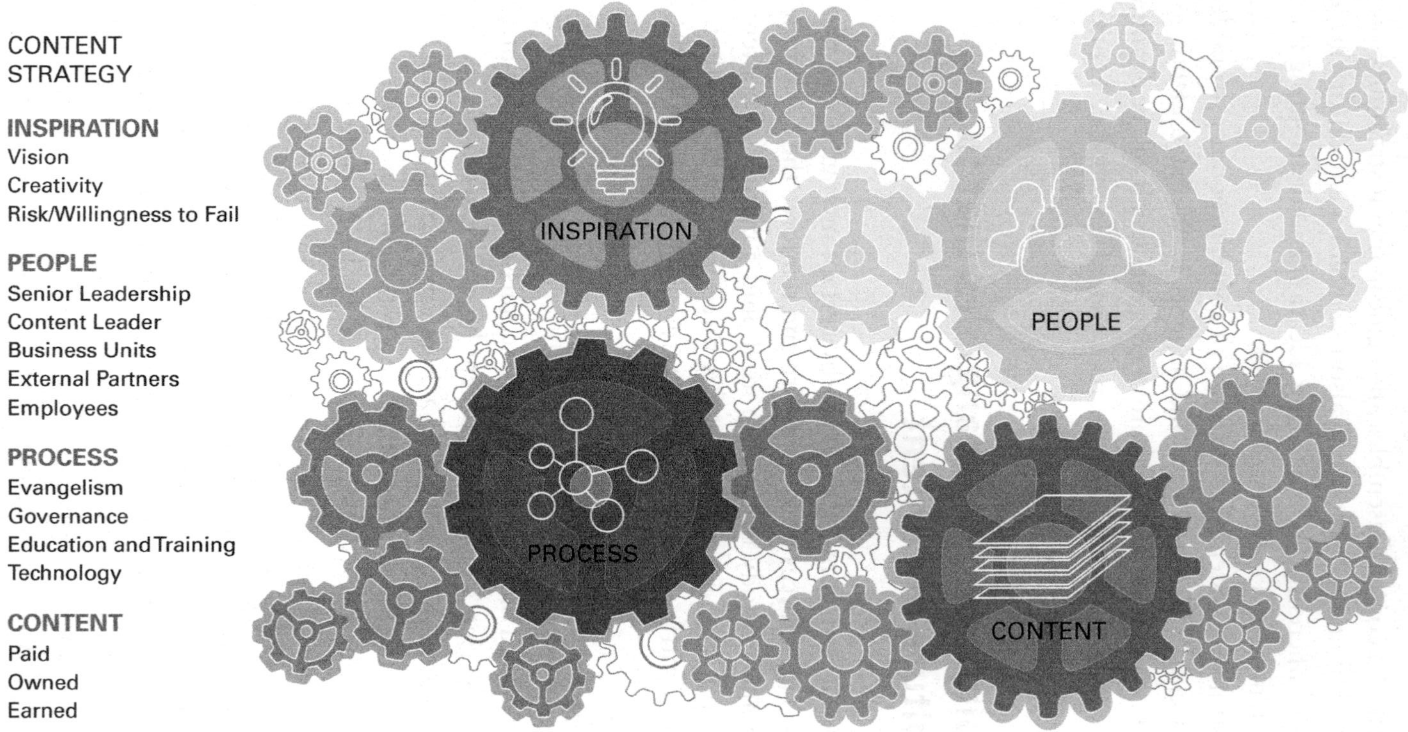
CONTENT
STRATEGY
INSPIRATION
Vision
Creativity
Risk/Willingness to Fail
PEOPLE
Senior Leadership
Content Leader
Business Units
External Partners
Employees
PROCESS
Evangelism
Governance
Education and Training
Technology
CONTENT
Paid
Owned
Earned
INSPIRATION
PEOPLE
PROCESS
CONTENT

SOURCE 'A culture of content', Rebecca Lieb and Jessica Groopman, Altimeter Group (2014) donate – its content objective is to inspire, educate and build relationships. It invests in talent to execute high-quality creative, as well as investing in ways to inspire that talent. charity: water gauges content success on the basis of inspiration, known internally as an 'inspiration quotient' – that is, did the content inspire its audience?

While not a formalized metric, charity: water's former Director of Digital, Paull Young, cites Seattle-based EastLake Community Church as an example. Inspired by charity: water's content and mission, the church created a content and event series that raised more than $709,000, enough to provide 54,541 Cambodians with access to clean water, well exceeding its fundraising goal. The church now includes clean water as a ministry budget line item and donates $5 to charity: water in honour of every first-time church visitor.[2]

Creativity

Organizations can also inspire a culture of content by thinking beyond traditional marketing tactics that have worked in the past. Training organizations to creatively think about and produce content serves two ends. First, it helps differentiate the organization through its content, an increasingly important tactic in a crowded and noisy media environment. Second, it grants the very individuals who create content (eg designers, copywriters, bloggers, videographers) the freedom to flex their creative muscles to reach current and new audiences.

Creativity flourishes most with multiple perspectives and, as such, customers can serve as an inspirational source for creative content. Content marketers (among other business functions) can leverage both earned media and listening analytics across all media to extract insights on how to evolve existing artefacts and justify new approaches.

Risk and a willingness to fail

Risk and a willingness to fail emerged repeatedly in our research as a critical force for empowering a culture of content. Providing permission to fail and assurance mitigates such fear as fear of failure, embarrassment and job termination – fundamental obstacles to the creative process. Strong content is valuable; it informs, educates, entertains or solves a problem. To differentiate through any one of these uses, content marketers must be comfortable with and empowered to take risks, to fail entirely and to move forward, applying learnings from failure.

Even massive, global corporations with multiple lines of business view risk taking as critical to differentiation, employee empowerment, market share growth and scale. Gurdeep Dhillon, global VP of audience engagement marketing at SAP, points to the willingness to fail as a driver of culture. He encourages his team to recognize, learn from and move on from failures quickly and with a spirit of innovation.

People: the human foundation of a culture of content

No tool or technology is as essential to a culture of content as people. A culture is, after all, common beliefs, practices, attitudes and behaviours that are shared by a group. And just like in other types of cultures, in an organization's culture some people have more influence than others. In an organization, hierarchies, divisions and external partners (eg agencies and vendors) each play a role in the culture of content.

Senior leadership

C-level executives do not tend to implement a culture of content, but their buy-in and evangelism can be critical to driving success and adoption throughout the enterprise. Staff at enterprises including GE and Johnson & Johnson cite CMOs with an expressed passion for content as integral to the entire spectrum of their marketing programmes.

When that passion is lacking or must be developed, many marketing executives make a formal business case to management to encourage them to adopt and finance content initiatives. Content leaders cite metrics as a frequent point of entry. SAP began its content initiatives by launching small, inexpensive, and carefully monitored and measured programmes so the C-suite could be approached with tangible, actionable results. This is not a one-time pitch but a constant, ongoing process.

Content leader

Whether content and its culture require a dedicated leader is a still-evolving conversation. Similarly evolving is the breadth of authority that a leader wields, such as global, departmental or regional. As a result, the much-vaunted 'chief content officer' is a role that exists in precious few organizations.

As we discussed in Chapter 5, there is a marked preference for a content leader, but whether that person's authority is limited to a department, location or region, or has a global purview, is highly inconsistent. A content leader's foremost responsibilities include evangelizing and constantly demonstrating content's value, creating a content strategy, putting processes and infrastructure into place, and driving interdepartmental coordination and awareness. More than any other role, including senior management, the content leader gets everyone on the same page.

The content leader also creates a sense of content ownership within specific business units or divisions. The leader articulates the importance of content, detects cross-functional areas where content is needed, spots and nurtures creative talent, and identifies individuals in the organization who share a content-centric mindset.

Business units

A defining characteristic of a culture of content is that content travels a circulatory system that goes beyond marketing to permeate other divisions. Clearly, communications, PR, social media, marketing teams and other divisions participate in content initiatives because they rely on content to communicate at scale. What other divisions to include, and how to prioritize their inclusion, naturally differs from business to business but, not surprisingly, our research found that customer-facing groups are cited as mandatory participants.

Groups include customer support and sales in B2C organizations, as well as thought leadership and subject-matter experts from among senior executives, researchers and often product groups. Legal is frequently part of the approval and governance process, and IT must advise on software and tools integration and deployment. To motivate these groups, avoid asking them to work for marketing. Instead, tie content to individual or departmental objectives, and develop metrics that enable them to track their progress towards these goals.

External partners

Smaller organizations, such as charity: water, argue that content is more passionate, authentic and human when it is homegrown. For larger brands facing issues of scale, however, external partners are a necessity; for some, it can be akin to the necessity of scaling content outside the marketing organization. Equally urgent is the need for cultural unity among all parties.

Kraft works with several agencies, including MXM, Starcom, TBWA, 360i and McGarryBowen. In addition, it partners with shopper marketing and insights organizations to help retailers better sell their products. Central to these many initiatives and partnerships is a social media monitoring centre that examines activity around individual brands with a variety of lenses for insights by segment, geolocation and influencers.

Another brand extending its partnerships is Nestlé, which is using outside relationships to foster more creativity and experimentation. Mondelēz also seeks partners to create enough content to steadily feed to media and social channels, a capacity that B Bonin Bough, former chief media and e-commerce officer, says does not exist in-house. Bough's mantra? 'Find the thing that works, and operationalize it.'

Employees

There is no consistent framework for bringing individual employees into a content culture, but there are best practices. Evangelism can help pinpoint hand-raisers and enthusiastic contributors. Not all contributors will be content creators, but employees can be encouraged and empowered to identify content needs or stories worth spreading. If customer support, for example, continually sees people struggle with a setting on a device, or if sales sees a knowledge gap that interrupts the funnel, the ability for them to flag a content need for an appropriate leader or team can prove valuable.

Training, educating, demonstrating value and welcoming feedback and input are essential to this flow of input and information. Many organizations are operationalizing this via internal social networks, highlighting best practices, case studies, feedback solicitation and asset sharing. Digital acceleration teams are another way to inspire and encourage participation in content initiatives, as are centres of excellence.

We predict that companies that foster a strong culture of content will increasingly make content part of the hiring process. This will not be based so much on aptitude (eg a talent for writing) as attitude; an enthusiasm for participation, storytelling, sharing or otherwise contributing to the content process.

Process: components that streamline and scale a culture of content

Establishing clear processes, roles and resources helps a culture of content to thrive and evolve over time. It's the oil in the well-oiled engine that a culture of content embodies (see Figure 6.2). The content's governing body creates that oil, helping the engine to run more efficiently. When the governing body develops strategic alignment, workflow and process clarity, consistent tools, guidelines and triage protocols, as well as identify stakeholders, it empowers employees to ideate, create, approve, disseminate, measure, optimize and scale content more efficiently.

The fuel for all of this, though, is a relentless crusade to demonstrate the unique value of content to every aspect of the organization.

Figure 6.2   A culture of content flows outwards across the organization

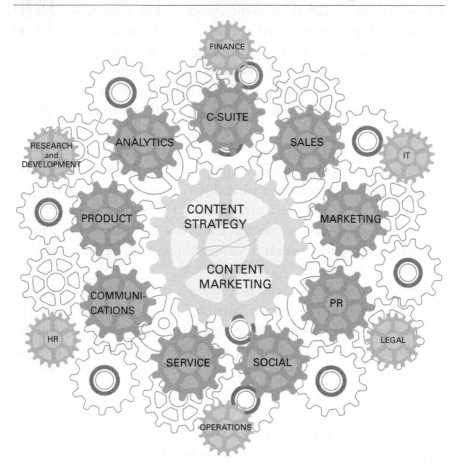

SOURCE 'A culture of content', Rebecca Lieb and Jessica Groopman, Altimeter Group (2014)

Evangelism

A culture of content does not just produce content, it truly values it. Thus evangelism, education and training are foundational, because if stakeholders do not understand a content strategy's purpose or process, they have little incentive to embrace it. Defining the value that content generates across business functions, and aligning that value to business objectives, are central to gaining buy-in at every level in the organization. Content marketing leaders must identify and build relationships with other functional leaders, and not just once, but continuously, fostering deeper understanding, value and trust over time.

Many organizations begin evangelizing the content's value at the consumer-facing level, citing marketing, corporate communications and customer service as primary candidates for buy-in. Salesforce.com deems the end user of any specific piece of content as the owner of that content. Thus, the most frequent content needs are in customer service, social media and sales, but also extend outwards to product development, R&D, HR, IT and beyond. Content evangelists listen for and leverage department-specific pain points and day-to-day needs as a way to create cross-functional justification and buy-in for content investment.

Both B2B and B2C organizations involve marketing and other consumer-facing roles initially, later pushing into less consumer-facing roles based on frequency of content needs, as outlined above. Companies must also involve external partners, including agencies, vendors and research organizations. The key to evangelism is understanding the unique needs and pain points of each constituency, and tailoring content initiatives to serve their needs and yield relevant results to drive greater buy-in.

Governance

Establishing clear guidelines for who does what and when creates structure and clarity in the content marketing programme. Specifically, the governing body (eg centre of excellence, editorial board, steering committee) defines how content is developed, curated, created and reviewed; what the brand guidelines are; what the standards for content artefacts are; who is empowered to make editorial decisions; and how to manage crises. Governance empowers employees to act autonomously while also making decisions in line with the organization, whether acting on behalf of headquarters or across international borders. Governance also helps organizations to manage workflows, accountability, safeguards, and the like, for distributing content publication responsibilities across multiple departments and levels. To enable a culture of content, the governing body must ensure that content is accessible across business functions and represents cross-functional needs.

Education and training

When new programmes are rolled out, initial educational programmes are key to access and adoption, but training must be ongoing to share best practices and updates on programmes, tools and workflows. Training can range from formal face-to-face sessions to less formalized programmes through the content centre of excellence and evangelism by programme leaders.

While there may be one overarching leader, many brands also designate regional or departmental leaders to support training at scale. Many enterprises also focus on enabling less formal, more routine knowledge sharing through enterprise collaboration tools or internal social networks. Collaboration tools help connect and empower each role in the content marketing chain, from copywriters to legal to agencies, to benefit from and repurpose each other's efforts. Hiring or promoting with an eye for editorial or creative background, or even just enthusiasm and a willingness to participate in content initiatives, can help accelerate the learning curve.

Technology

As we will cover more in Chapter 10, the role of technology in a culture of content is to centralize, streamline and optimize. It is to provide a central tool set for execution, knowledge sharing, branded assets, approvals, analysis and reporting. Successfully leveraging content marketing (and any other) technology is a function of defining the organization's priority use cases and aligning the tools against those use cases, not the other way around.

Stakeholder alignment is important to success. Shared access to common tools that serve multiple teams helps streamline creation, curation, measurement, analytics and deployment. An editorial calendar, for example, is a simple but vital component for keeping stakeholders clear on publishing frequency, media types and publishing channels, as well as on the alignment of content cadence with the organization's larger content strategy. Analytics is also critical, as an integrated understanding of how paid, owned and earned content is performing across channels and platforms helps inform opportunities for optimization, more efficient spend, process effectiveness and, most importantly, identification of what resonates with specific audiences and in what context.

But tools are only as valuable as their level of integration, particularly when it comes to driving behavioural adoption, change and empowerment. Organizations must recognize the imperative to integrate systems (eg content management, digital asset management, social media management, advertising platforms, mobile management and agency systems) to drive as holistic a view of content performance and customer experience as possible – and not just create another silo.

Converged media results in content begetting more content

A primary impetus for a pervasive, unified culture of content is the growing knowledge and acceptance of the fact that content is the atomic particle of all marketing across paid, owned and earned channels, as we addressed in Chapter 3. Content is not just a company blog or newsletter. Instead, it is myriad forms of media that fuel social, PR and advertising. This new mindset is changing the make-up and structure of marketing organizations and going far to foster a culture of content in more mature organizations.

Nestlé explicitly designs content to function in advertising and social media. Media efficiency, according to Pete Blackshaw, global head of digital and social media at Nestlé, is creating the amount of value from earned media that equals the spend on paid. To that end, content must be buzzworthy and function in paid, owned and earned channels.

Both B2B and B2C organizations are working to eliminate internal barriers between content, media and data to create an exchange of ideas and a content circulatory system both within the enterprise and with external partners.

Organizations must create and systematize the integration of paid, owned and earned media with regularly scheduled meetings leading up to content activation. For example, three or four weeks before an initiative is deployed, all channel owners convene in a room to plan together. The following week, teams align and review individual plans on the best way to move forward, share assets, measure and redeploy in different channels and media. Such meetings are rarely about content per se but rather about seamless experiences that cross channels, media and devices.

Other content leaders design content to later slice into component parts. Package assets with a list of top-line points to make it easier for other teams to digest and apply content for use in other channels, such as social selling.

Success criteria

Our research finds common trends across companies that embody a culture of content. Content leaders must embrace the following criteria to help drive shared understanding, access and value of content across the enterprise:

- customer obsession guides content;
- align content with brand;
- drive content leadership from the top down and the bottom up;
- culture requires constant evangelism;
- test and learn;
- global must enable local;
- integrate across all cultural components.

Customer obsession guides content

An obsession with understanding customer wants, preferences, behaviours, trends and passions helps drive a culture of content because the data informs how brands use content to serve customers. Whether listening to customer feedback directly or monitoring customer interactions across various touch points, companies with a well-defined culture of content are equipped to optimize rapidly based on customer insights. This is embodied in the convergence of media, when paid, owned and earned must work together because the consumer sees only one brand, not specific departments. As such, content helps define the human side of a brand – creative, helpful, passionate, contextually sensitive, and even vulnerable.

Instead of letting editorial calendars dictate content cadence, Kraft asks what is worthy of distribution in the first place, based on how people spend their time. Kraft's standard of worthiness is a human way of determining what to publish, based on whether the content is worth customers spending their valuable time and attention. Kraft makes this decision by:

- listening for consumer insights across channels;
- designing content to unify the customer–brand experience;
- assessing all content for worthiness.

Align content with brand

Every company should have its own understanding of purpose, differentiation, philosophy and vision. While these will vary from company to company, brands must articulate how content serves those elements underlying the very identity of the brand. How content embodies brand values must be clear to every level, from the C-suite to functional leads to practitioners. This alignment should be a guiding force and benchmark for what constitutes worthy and authentic branded content. To align the content with the brand:

- crystallize how the content supports the brand vision;
- incorporate that vision into training and evangelism;
- only publish content that supports the brand vision.

Drive content leadership from the top down and the bottom up

The content leader must facilitate a top-down and a bottom-up approach to drive a culture of content. Top-down, C-level buy-in is critical not only for investment and programme expansion but also for leadership by example. Top-down content leadership helps drive investment and an understanding, a mentality, and enactment of the value of content across the company.

Simultaneously, a strong leader or advocate is nearly always required for education, evangelism, training and testing, which drives buy-in from the bottom up. Bottom-up content leadership can manifest through greater departmental buy-in, alignment, demand for content, and internal participation down to the practitioner level. As the value of content is translated across other business functions through evangelism and small, inexpensive programmes supporting those functions, hard numerical results aligning with business objectives help justify deeper executive support. To drive content leadership:

- Evangelize and test department-specific initiatives to drive bottom-up support.
- Leverage cross-functional results and support to drive top-down support.
- Both C-level and content leaders must reinforce an ongoing culture of content.

Culture requires constant evangelism

While culture is pervasive and powerful, it is not built overnight. It slowly gains acceptance and takes steady reinforcement. Terms such as 'constant', 'relentless', 'frequent' and 'reinforcement' are commonly used to describe a culture of content. Why? Because content leaders must constantly demonstrate business and consumer value across the organization. Recruiting and securing participation from divisions, groups and territories is based heavily on WIIFM ('what's in it for me?') and is demonstrated by metrics that relate to their goals. This evangelism must continue over time – through results, case studies, best (and worst) practice sharing, centrally shared tools and resources, and recycled content. To create a culture of content:

- Content leaders must lead the content evangelism.
- Articulate and demonstrate WIIFM, both bottom-up and top-down.
- Commit to ongoing cross-functional evangelism, support, communication and optimization.

Test and learn

Brands must be willing to take risks in the content they produce. This requires a spirit of piloting small, tightly scoped content initiatives with predetermined KPIs that align with business objectives. These initiatives, especially early on, do not necessarily have to be resource intensive. Testing and learning are less about new channel, device or content plays and more about creating ostensible business value that can be reported back to leadership in order to drive programme and resource expansion.

These tasks are inherent to a culture of content because they require taking risks, which may result in failure or in tangible justification to use when evangelizing content across functions and to leadership. To test content:

- Start with small, tightly scoped, inexpensive pilots.
- Listen, analyse, A/B test, optimize and repeat.
- Take risks, fail forwards and apply lessons.

Global must enable local

Whether you are a large multinational corporation with presences across dozens of countries, or a company with numerous locations in one country, a culture of content must be enabled locally. Divisional authority and autonomy with strategic oversight is as important for national companies as it is for multinational or international companies, because both must empower local practitioners with local content that reflects local tastes, context and language. This could be a case study suited for a German-speaking audience, or simply tweaking content by region based on weather or news, such as promoting snow tyres in New England and beach umbrellas in Florida. We will dive more into enabling global content marketing in Chapter 7.

As brands are forced to become publishers, enabling local authority is critical to standing out. To enable local:

- Global must provide strategic oversight, support, resources and direction.

- Enable local teams with appropriate cultural, linguistic and contextual resources.

- Appoint regional and/or local content leaders to scale training and ongoing evangelism.

Integrate across all cultural components

In a true culture of content, integration and shared insights should exist across every component of the culture: people, processes, mindsets and the content itself. Culture does not work in silos. Integrated workflows across teams, business units, and internal and external parties help streamline and scale content deployment. Integrated technology systems with shared access, reporting, data and automation enable agility and meaningful measurement. Even media itself, through the convergence of paid, owned and earned must be connected through workflow and divisional coordination, designed for optimizing resources. Integrate insights:

- Integrate across people: workflows, tool access, collaboration, best-practice sharing.

- Integrate across technology: data sets, systems, third-party tools, analytics.

- Integrate across media: paid, owned, earned, local, and so on.

As brands continue to embrace content as a valuable, inspired business asset that establishes essential points of differentiation, content strategy and content culture will deeply infuse organizational cultures. Content will become like other enterprise assets (eg financial, plants, data inventory) where organizational acceptance of key best practices will be well-defined, engendering wider accountability and ownership of the problem.

A culture of content ensures the viability of a unified brand experience; better, more contextually relevant and more timely interaction with customers and prospects; improved customer experiences; and the leveraging of the investments that companies are making in technology. The rewards of a culture of content for brands are far-reaching: stronger branding and identity, a greater share of voice, better and faster communications and resolutions, and boosts to all stages of the purchase funnel.

Notes

1   Chernov, J (2014) [accessed 6 January 2017] State of Inbound 2014, *Hubspot* [Online] https://cdn2.hubspot.net/hub/53/file-1589882006-pdf/HubSpot-State-of-Inbound-2014.pdf

2   Zellmer, S (2012) [accessed 6 January 2017] Campaign Update: Drinks4Drinks, *The Water Log* [Online] http://www.charitywater.org/blog/drinks4drinks

Global content strategy 07

Content marketing is ubiquitous, yet organizations find themselves challenged to scale operations. Operating and governing content initiatives across borders, cultures, regions and languages presents both strategic and tactical challenges, even to the best-resourced enterprises. Opportunities abound for organizations that can scale content marketing globally, ultimately providing better marketing opportunities, more efficient spend, synchronized teams and efficient workflow, all while enabling organizations to meet both micro and macro goals.

In other words? Content marketing is going to be big!

Creating a global content strategy is absolutely essential, and inherent to any content strategy for multinational organizations. At the same time, the more countries, regions, languages, staff, technologies, regulatory climates, vendors and partners that are involved, the more exponentially challenging it is to create that strategy. Without a conscious effort at orchestration, time and money are wasted, employees become frustrated, efforts are duplicative and customer experience suffers, not to mention consistency in brand and messaging.

The need for content is universal, yet each region, country and locality in which a brand operates has diverse and specific needs unique to language and culture, and often other requirements, such as legalities. Fundamentally, these needs can be divided into three buckets that are core components of any content strategy: teams, tools and channels. We will explore these challenges more in this chapter, as well as the processes, organization models and resources needed to bring opportunities to fruition.

Overcoming the challenges of global content marketing

Enterprises are quickly realizing that content must permeate the entire organization. This applies globally just as much as it does regionally, but scaling content up to a global level brings with it a host of additional challenges, as set out below.

Teams

Global content marketing requires centralized leadership, but also a very substantial degree of local authority and autonomy. If there is a parallel editorial model, it would be that of a major international news organization. The New York Times, CNN, the BBC and their ilk are centralized organizations with global headquarters, but all maintain bureaus in major regions and/or capitals across the world.

How regional and/or local leadership is appropriated, however, varies greatly. Very few organizations have formal content marketing departments or divisions. This is no less true of global enterprises that often assign content duties to marketing teams, social media groups or to communications/PR staff. Our research has identified six real-world content governance models (refer back to Chapter 5), all of which are as relevant to global content management as they are to running content strictly on a local or national basis.

Tools

The content marketing software landscape is rapidly evolving and shifting, as we will dive into more in Chapter 9. Selecting tools comes with additional considerations and concerns when they must serve global teams, including:

- Does the tool support multiple languages? Diverse alphabets?
- Can it handle country- (or region-) specific barriers, such as firewalls, popular local channels (eg Weibo in China, or Vk.com in Russia), or local privacy and data protection regulations?

- Will licences differ on a country-by-country basis?
- How easy (or difficult) will it be to train and onboard far-flung users?
- Can the solution be integrated with other marketing and enterprise software already in use (or planned for deployment) on a global or regional level?

Our recent research on the content software landscape finds 40 per cent of marketers cite a lack of interdepartmental coordination as leading to investment in disparate, incompatible tool sets. And that is just on a domestic level. Global requirement demands attention be paid to sharing, collaboration and efficiency.

At Dell, a high level of collaboration is required among many teams before content can go to market. This can result in challenges around workflow and approval process, with too many 'cooks in the kitchen'. Global Digital Marketing Strategy Lead Nicole Mills told us, 'We're challenged in sharing information across all teams; it's a visibility issue. There's an audit trail of when changes are happening during the approval cycle. The complexity of the company contributes to a complicated workflow in order to meet everyone's needs.' This can result in inefficiencies from creation to publication.

Channels

What content should be created? Where should it be published, and in what form, and for which audience? Publishing on Facebook simply is not the same as engaging with social audiences on Vk.com, Line, Mixi or Weibo. Quality control of content from one channel to the next, across regions, can also be challenging.

> 'We do a great job of sharing content today among channels and accounts. The challenge is to get it seen, now that all the algorithms keep changing. We have paid media programmes as well, so media buying effectiveness is priority too.'
>
> *Chris Murphy, Adidas*

Additionally, there are regional holidays to consider, local sporting events (in most of the rest of the world, for example, 'football' means 'soccer'), festivals, superstitions, political and news happenings and concerns, and more. Throw real-time marketing into the mix, and you are required to adhere to even more country-specific documentation and processes per channel, as less can be left to chance. Ignore these differences and you are instantly an outsider, not a credible source of information or a potential partner.

Local input, local knowledge and an injection of local culture are all essential. It is not nearly enough to translate content into a local language, or to push content created at headquarters out into regional divisions. In fact, often the content created or surfaced in faraway markets can bubble up as fodder for headquarters, or for other markets.

Setting the foundation with the right people

No tool or technology is as essential to executing a global content strategy successfully as people. In an organization, hierarchies, divisions and external partners (eg agencies and vendors) each play a role in the culture of content.

Executives

Change on a global scale must begin with the C-suite and other upper-management leaders. Without executive support, across regions and with a global view, content strategy remains unconnected, as each country and/or region operates in their own silo with no mandate for coordination. Senior leaders must buy in to the need for global content strategy and evangelize accordingly throughout the organization.

But how can change agents get the blessing of executives if no formal business case has been made? Focus on metrics as the starting point. Examine successful content marketing initiatives that have been implemented in multiple markets, as well as those that have failed due to lack of coordination. Zero in on precise elements of country- or region-specific content strategies that could be reappropriated elsewhere in the enterprise to positively impact key metrics such as sales, brand lift and customer satisfaction. Data is your best ally to get global content strategy on the radar of senior leaders.

> 'Exploit the mutually felt pain points to make the business case for a global content strategy. When you have agreement around pain points, there's desire to make changes.'
>
> *Susan Ridge, Save the Children*

Content leaders

As discussed in Chapter 6 on building a culture of content, the content leader must facilitate a top-down and a bottom-up approach to drive change. The content leader may be the elusive chief content officer, or a senior leader in marketing, digital, social or PR/communications. The key responsibilities of this role are to constantly evangelize and demonstrate content's value; create content strategy; implement processes and infrastructure; coordinate across departments and build ownership; identify gaps, needs and opportunities; and nurture creative talents and content-centric mindsets.

Employees

Though not all employees will be content creators, all can be encouraged and empowered to be content identifiers. This empowerment comes from leadership evangelizing the importance of content on a global scale, and providing sufficient training and education around how to identify content fodder. Operationalize content gathering and submissions via internal social networks, wherein best (and worst) practices should be highlighted through case studies, feedback sharing and asset sharing. When hiring, HR teams should incorporate content needs into job descriptions and talent searches.

> 'You need to get all teams thinking globally the second they have an idea for a new piece of content. Because, once you get creative, you tend to be content marketing-centric in getting it out the door. If you then have to make global considerations for every market, it will take longer, and the deadline will be further extended.'
>
> *Jason Miller, global content marketing leader at LinkedIn*

External partners

As you are aligning internal employees and teams around a global content strategy, it is also important to consider the need for external partners to help with content creation. Look at agencies of all kinds and sizes, as content expertise now permeates vendors from the niche content houses to marketing insights organizations. It is typical for today's savvy content marketer to work with a variety of boutique content partners in emerging markets, shying away from the typical 'agency of record' model from the paid advertising days of yore. Why? Because, according to IBM, content requires different agency skill sets and can be best served by local resources for smaller markets. We also found that agencies can be useful on a global scale in side-stepping legal review of creative, as they assume responsibility.

Streamlining and scaling global content strategy

Content is a team sport, and coordinating content on a global scale is a bit like running the Olympic Games. Each region must have teams, those teams must have captains, and they must be equipped with training, an understanding of the universal rules of the game, and also be equipped with the equipment needed to play the game. Yet, at the same time, each team will always fly its own flag, and proudly wear its own colours.

To get there requires an intense concentration on change management. Global content strategy is as much of a change management issue as a process one. People are used to operating with their own production and communications schedule, and it can be difficult to get them to think globally. Global enterprises must organize under the right governance model, adequately resource content production and execution, and ensure seamless and efficient collaboration with the right tool set in order to effectively scale country- and region-specific content strategies to a global level.

'To achieve efficiencies in global content marketing, companies must prioritize upfront planning, development of global work-streams and potential costs of operational infrastructure. Without these considerations, the attempt to "go global" will fail.'

Sherri Chien-Niclas, formerly at Symantec

Organizational governance dictates how content will flow among countries/regions. In our research, we uncovered that organizations most often facilitate global content strategy via a global brand group (eg 3M) or a central content group (eg Intel). These models typically strategize via global region rather than individual country, though large countries (or those with geographical significance) are often viewed independently. Large countries also house prominent content leaders within their country or region, such as a chief content officer, or similar.

In an effort to break down brand silos that led to inefficiencies and overlap in customer engagement, Marriott International has created a centralized content and creative group that all of its 30 brands report to. Within that group, there are three divisions: 1. Creative Agency (key cards, print collateral, invoices); 2. Content Studio (anything story-driven such as films, webisodes, magazines, books, TV shows and social content); 3. M Live (real-time marketing team that handles social engagement with consumers). This structure exists in the United States and other markets globally too (London, Dubai and Miami), with their reports answering to the United States as well as their content leadership locally.

Other best practices for governing global content strategy include:

- Keep it lean to avoid being 'bogged down' by approvals and too many people wanting input on content. Follow the example of

IBM's Diamond Team agile organizational model. They are able to execute a project quickly, with the right people from varied disciplines at the table (analytics, product marketing, portfolio marketing head, a designer and a social expert), who are used to working with each other efficiently. Intel also has a dedicated governance team that specializes in approval processes and knows what channels to use, when. This enables constant review and adaptation to emerging content needs.

- Apply lessons learned from one market to other areas of opportunity. We found in our research that mature global enterprises build a strong content engine in one market (typically their largest, most resourced country or region), then use those learnings from both success and failure to further another market. LinkedIn even moved its content lead, Jason Miller, from the United States to the United Kingdom to use his talent to solve new challenges.

- Content teams should also have a direct connection to legal in order to avoid any potential litigation further down the road. Have clear policies in place during content sourcing, creation and dissemination – with appropriate checks and balances with legal – to ensure efficient strategy execution among all involved. Regular briefings among leaders from regional/country teams are also effective to ensure alignment and raise any potential red flags before they make an impact.

Budget constraints lead to content advantages from one region to the next. Though cross-region collaboration is occurring in most global organizations, cross-region resource allocation is not equal. Not every global region has the same budget to allocate towards content marketing employees, partners and media buys, leaving some at an advantage over others in creativity and creation abilities. At Brand Publis, the content budget comes from the worldwide group, and is distributed as needed to go-to-market teams. Governance processes manage how that money is doled out, when and why.

Save the Children is attempting to better understand the budget needs of its members (regions and countries) by conducting an audit of the processes behind content gathering and curation. What expenditures are undertaken by each member? Susan Ridge, chief marketing officer, elaborates: 'It has been a massive undertaking, but a major step in the right direction. We looked at how many trips they are making per year to gather content, how much is spent on vendors, and the balance investment and ROI. This audit created a baseline across the globe and exposed levels of maturity in different members, ultimately contributing to creating a culture of content.'

Organizations can level the playing field – at least, partially – by offering customizable foundation content at the 'hub' level. This content can easily be repurposed by each country or region and aligns with the overall global content strategy and goals. It is also critical to set concrete objectives and KPIs for each country/regional office with fewer resources, in order to set expectations and maintain efficiencies when they are juggling multiple priorities and responsibilities. Finally, organizations must dedicate full-time resources (content leaders) to manage more than one region in order to scale globally.

> 'All content power cannot come from one region with no one lighting a fire elsewhere.'
>
> *Jason Miller, LinkedIn*

Collaboration tools aid in planning and executing a global content strategy. With miles of land and ocean among country offices and regional centres, it can be painstaking to ensure collaboration and alignment of content teams. Thankfully, a slew of collaboration technologies are available to aid in communication, asset sharing and process alignment for global enterprises. Skip on to Chapter 9 to learn more about your software options, including digital asset management (DAM) software; utilizing current customer relationship management (CRM) databases for discussion, such as Salesforce.com; and other tools to help your teams and their strategies to remain connected.

Content software is a big investment, and takes a lot of time to migrate from existing legacy systems. Save the Children International is proving value in its new system by migrating its largest members, the United States and United Kingdom, first, before rolling out the platform to all its global members. Dell approaches changes through review by its global marketing technology team that provides oversight to content needs in various geographies, coordinating technology use and rollout.

Global content strategy success factors

Through our research, we uncovered eight success factors that enable organizations to effectively scale content strategy across the globe:

1 strategy and vision;

2 business unit collaboration;

3 localization;

4 hiring and empowering talent;

5 willingness to take risks;

6 content evangelism;

7 education and training;

8 technology adoption.

Strategy and vision

As reviewed in the previous chapter, a culture of content has to commit to being global in all processes, in every market, and plan for timelines and dissemination schedules accordingly. At the foundation of a culture of content lies a shared, single purpose, mission and goals that are paramount to empowering all employees to embrace a global content strategy. A strong vision is most effective when generated, embodied and exemplified by leadership first, though grass-roots efforts are also critical in building groundswell.

This vision establishes a baseline of understanding, connecting day-to-day content tasks to a higher purpose – one often tied to both content strategy and bettering the customer experience, as building community with consumers will ultimately fill the content pipeline through engagement and earned media. Alignment around core customer personas used for targeting and messaging – as well as overarching customer experience (CX) goals – is critical, as it sets the foundation for localization at the regional level.

> 'It is difficult to develop global personas; they are too generic. Persona development and journey mapping working on a more localized level is essential.'
>
> *Piers Dickinson, DuPont*

Business unit collaboration

Seasoned content strategy leaders understand that content travels far beyond the marketing department, permeating other divisions (consumer-facing, first). Enable collaboration among your organization's branding, PR, communications, social media, sales, HR, R&D, customer support and field marketing teams. At Adidas, they loop PR into content activities from a communications standpoint, as it is part of one of Adidas's nine internal 'newsrooms' across the globe. Each newsroom network works together as a global team to increase earned social coverage, as well as drive earned media.

Legal and IT are typically involved as well, more on the side of approvals, governance, and technology implementation and deployment. Also involve subject-matter experts in formulating and maintaining your global content strategy, dispersing them among senior executives, researchers and product groups.

From our interviews, we uncovered that collaboration is most successful when approached from two forms of communication: collaboration tools and platforms (as discussed earlier in this chapter), and good old-fashioned phone calls! We heard time and time again that the best way to get something done is to simply pick up the phone. Do it often, on a regular basis, in addition to using collaboration and asset-sharing software to keep the content engine running. Tools are also helpful in planning and scheduling content in a universal editorial calendar that can be used to ensure cross-country consistency, as well as content tracking, enforcement and measurement.

In 2013, Unilever invested in a single tool to consolidate and coordinate content creation and publishing efforts across just three brands in the dozens of countries in which it operates (not to mention use and collaboration for hundreds of internal and external content stakeholders: staff, agency and vendor partners). The brand realized $10 million savings in just one year.

Localization

Global teams ensure scale and cross-geography strategy implementation, while local teams are responsible for actual content creation based on market knowledge. Content creation at the regional or country level is often dependent on and adapted from 'anchor' content that is centrally created and addresses issues/topics that affect all regions. However, global content will not fulfil all regional needs, and all relevant geographies must be adequately resourced if expected to contribute content.

Set clear global guidelines for content that is expected of regions, including guidance on customer messaging structure and connection to overarching strategic goals. Localization guidelines should both empower creators, while also taking into account country-specific regulations. Remember to keep these guidelines as lean as possible, as language translation and legal reapproval needs can quickly add complexity.

Marriott International has reaped the rewards of localized content that enables its customers to envision themselves in new destinations. David Beebe, VP of global creative and content marketing, shares: 'Destination content puts heads in beds. Our "French Kiss" promotion drove $550,000 in sales for that hotel when it opened, as we offered packages to visit French locations. In the first 90 days, we booked 7,200 rooms.'

Hiring and empowering talent

We see two distinct hiring trends emerging among companies that are building and growing their global content strategies: they either hire more specific domain expertise, or go the opposite route and hire more generalists. The route you choose will depend on the amount of technical or cultural expertise you require regionally, as well as the talent you need to build your strategy team at the global level. Also look for potential hires with an editorial or creative background in order to accelerate the learning curve once they are in a content role.

According to Bob Meindl, content marketing director at Cisco, niche subject-matter expertise should be shared among regions by laddering it up to a global group that then disseminates it to other country content efforts. At Bosch, they hire content generalists who are given specific responsibilities once assigned to a team. This aligns with an agile methodology that increases efficiencies by filling in resources as dictated by immediate needs that are constantly shifting and reprioritizing.

Refer back to the section on building content teams earlier in the chapter for additional hiring and team-building recommendations.

Willingness to take risks

To differentiate through content, content marketers must be empowered to take risks. This empowerment comes from leadership that provides permission to fail. In turn, employees no longer feel failure, embarrassment or the threat of job termination for innovating. Instead they recognize the issue that may have occurred from taking a content risk, learn from it and quickly move on. More content leaders are incorporating risk-taking attributes and willingness to fail into the hiring process.

> 'There needs to be a global entity that really thinks about the next big step in marketing and customer experience. How will you take risks and test new approaches in content, formats, etc?'
>
> *Jeff Ramminger, Brand Publis*

Evangelism

The key to evangelism is understanding the unique needs and pains of each constituency and tailoring content initiatives to serve their needs and yield relevant results to drive greater buy-in. Global content marketing leaders must continuously identify and build relationships with other functional content leaders at the region and country level. This includes all external partners, both those used globally and regionally. Internal evangelism across departments is also important. In our research, we find that many companies begin evangelism across consumer-facing departments first, as content strategies are increasingly focused on bettering CX.

Education and training

Content training must be both initial and ongoing, and should include a combination of best-practice sharing, case examples from the industry and competitors, updates on programmes and workflows, and more formal classes or workshops. For example, IBM brings in screenwriters and White House speechwriters to teach storytelling. Dell has followed suit, as its global digital marketing strategy lead Nicole Smith shares: 'It takes formal training to become a good storyteller, especially in a global organization where content marketers are likely coming from varied disciplines and levels of marketing expertise.'

> 'Brands executing content marketing on a global scale must think, operate and hire like a publisher, as that is who they are competing with for customer eyeballs and engagement.'
>
> Luke Kintigh, Intel

Training topics should also cover new types of content and channels, as well as any other types of expertise that will be required for transitioning legacy employees into content roles. We have seen this take the form of a 'Digital Marketing 101' course, offered to employees who need to build new skills as the company evolves.

Educational offerings must account for global, regional and local content programmes. In order for content marketing to permeate the culture of an organization, leadership must also make training mandatory and attach it to employee pay/bonus structure for maximum motivation. If you focus training solely on legal/regulatory compliance around content, not the crux of strategy and the skills needed to effectively perform roles, then participation and empowerment will be low.

Technology adoption

Within this chapter we have discussed how the right technologies choices can boost both collaboration among content leaders and strategists, as well as contribute to efficiencies in the content planning, creation, distribution and measurement process. Additional implications to consider when adopting the right tool(s) for the job include:

- Who owns the marketing stack? Does it include content efforts?
- Does the content group have input and requirement scoping before decisions are made?
- How will the technology be rolled out globally?
- Does the platform fulfil our priority needs (eg taxonomy classification, editorial calendaring, etc)?

At Cisco, they track content performance against 20 metrics in an engagement platform. Still, it can be difficult to attribute a sales-qualified lead to one piece of content, as not everything results in a lead on the day of customer interaction. Engagement is easy to prove with content technologies as they exist today, while ROI is not always as smooth sailing. Focus on metrics in the top, middle and bottom of the funnel to pinpoint growth/decline trends by channel, campaign and region over time, rather than attempting to zero in on the impact of one piece of content. We will explore content measurement more in Chapter 10.

Real-time marketing

08

Real-time marketing (RTM), the strategy and practice of reacting with immediacy in digital channels to external events and triggers, has been steadily growing in use and popularity. An expanding array of tools and digital channels (eg social media and listening capabilities) has made real-time accessible, in theory at least, to virtually every marketer. As digital channels become increasingly more real time, all marketing organizations must consider to what degree they, too, will function in real time.

Successful RTM requires enormous strategic and tactical preparation. This chapter explains the benefits of RTM, outlines the business cases to which it can be applied, and identifies the best practices and steps necessary to move an enterprise towards RTM readiness.

The benefits and challenges of RTM

We define RTM as the strategy and practice of responding with immediacy to external events and triggers. It is arguably the most relevant form of marketing, achieved by listening to and/or anticipating consumer interests and needs.

RTM has been entrenched in the digital arsenal for well over a decade. Triggered e-mail messaging is already used in 62 per cent of RTM strategies,[1] and search results, search advertisements and ad retargeting are other likely components of a marketer's existing RTM arsenal. However, the current trend in RTM is considerably more human and less automated. It is worth noting in this context that two forms of RTM are emerging: one that is entirely hand-crafted and the other sparked by increasingly sophisticated digital triggers. All RTM is deeply rooted in both content and social strategy.

The benefits of RTM span the business and consumer sectors. At one end, it supports the individual through hyper-personalization, customization, surprise and delight – and at the other end it serves the brand, as companies enjoy tremendous media buzz, increased following and positive sentiment. Specific benefits of RTM include:

- *Surprise and delight.* This is the feeling an individual has as the result of a more human (less corporate) interaction, the semblance of spontaneity, dialogue and brand interest in the individual.

- *The right message at the right time.* This is the ability to reach audiences with timely engagement throughout the customer journey, greater relevance, resonance and personalization.

- *Brand relevance.* This is the opportunity for brands to actually be cool. When brands do this right, they effectively tap into the zeitgeist, bridging brand relevance with what is hip and trendy. Consider the tremendous resonance of Oreo's now-infamous tweet: 'You can still dunk in the dark', both in social and traditional media, when the lights went out at the 2013 Super Bowl.

- *Always-on.* Participating in RTM enables brands to appear always on, available and listening through evergreen content, thought leadership and excellent customer service. Today's customers expect brands to respond swiftly, with 53 per cent expecting answers on Twitter in less than an hour (this rises to 72 per cent if lodging a complaint).[2]

RTM is also known to lift literally all desirable marketing metrics (eg interest, consideration, search, word-of-mouth, media receptivity, etc), as well as to turbo-charge other marketing initiatives.[3] Of companies utilizing RTM, 58 per cent attribute more than 40 per cent of their marketing budgets to it, and nearly 6 in 10 intend to increase that spending in 2016.[4] The movement towards RTM is being driven in part by consumer expectations for immediacy, relevance, and access increase with technology.

Yet while RTM comes with real benefits, so too are its many challenges. The first are plotting strategy and analysis. The potential for risk is greater in RTM, given the (near) immediate nature of interactions and posts. Brands must take extra precaution – planning and listening – in order to mitigate these risks.

The other set of challenges are in execution and organization. Speed, agility, scale, approvals, legalities, technology, analytics and the ability to deploy teams around the clock are daunting – not to mention expensive – prospects for many organizations. From an organizational standpoint, RTM can be confusing; it can be planning and resource-intensive and requires immense preparation and coordination. Many companies will grapple with approvals, particularly those in regulated industries.

RTM requires a shift in mindset: brands are relinquishing a measure of control in exchange for more opportunities for relevance and deeper, more personalized customer experiences. 'A lot of organizations are not comfortable with this concept of real time', explains Chad Warren, head of social and content marketing, digital marketing, at Adobe. 'Culturally, we're about reviewing and scrubbing, and generally quite guarded in how we present ourselves in front of the public. There has to be a recognition that we don't control the conversation any more as brands, and real-time marketing helps stakeholders to understand that and how we can still harness it.'

Six use cases of RTM

To better understand just what RTM is, and is not, we have identified six business use cases for RTM. These six use cases fall into two axes of RTM: 1) reactive and proactive; and 2) planned and unplanned (see Figure 8.1). Organizations will maintain the most control and can expect the best results from RTM when their efforts fall in the planned/proactive sector of the RTM quadrant. Use cases are discussed within this chapter in order – from the lowest degrees of planning and preparation needed to the highest.

Figure 8.1   The six use cases of real-time marketing

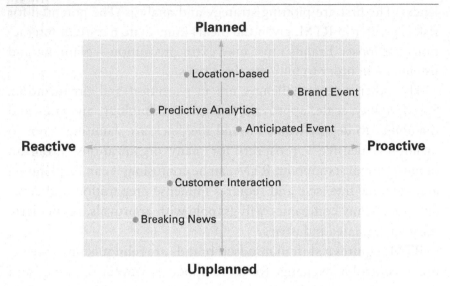

SOURCE 'Real-time marketing: the agility to leverage "now"', Rebecca Lieb, Altimeter Group (2013)

Use case 1: brand events

Close to 55 per cent of companies utilizing RTM do so for event promotion.[5] Examples of brand events include product launches, conferences, and media and customer-facing events where content strategy, pre-approvals, media and channel plans, hashtags, creative elements, editorial calendars, etc, can all be prepared in advance. During these events, staff are available to push out announcements and react to anticipated posts in social media. There should be few surprises in these planned brand events, but it should feel fresh and authentic rather than canned in advance.

Some examples include:

- When Samsung sponsored the 2012 Olympics, the electronics brand created experiences at various London landmarks dubbed 'Samsung Studios', which focused on demonstrating the newly released Galaxy S3 and Galaxy Note. Visitors could test the devices, print personalized badges and enter into a contest to win various prizes. The sponsored spaces resulted in 9 out of 10 visitors claiming they were more likely to consider a Samsung phone as a result of their Samsung Studio experience.[6]

Figure 8.2 Prop dragon skull on a beach to promote new *Game of Thrones* season available for streaming

SOURCE Blinkbox

- AMEX sponsors Small Business Saturday, a US event benefitting millions of small businesses, in which AMEX helps small, local businesses to prepare for marketing in real time prior to the event, by providing shops with tools, signage, templates and more, as well as offering rebates to customers who use their AMEX cards when purchasing.[7]

- When *Game of Thrones* Season 3 went live on UK streaming service Blinkbox, the company placed a 'dragon's skull' (see Figure 8.2) on a Dorset beach to spark attention (and 250 instances of press coverage). This resulted in a 632 per cent year-over-year revenue increase.[8]

Use case 2: anticipated events

A growing number of organizations have become mature enough to prepare for real-time events that can be anticipated in advance to fully leverage opportunities. Like with branded events, above, they prepare by having business goals, strategies, teams and approvals all done in advance, and they have content at the ready. This 'locked and loaded' approach is deployed by advertisers and sponsors (brands) in advance of major events not of their own making, such as the Super Bowl and award shows. Some examples include the following:

- During the 2013 Oscar awards, hair-care brand Pantene tweeted illustrations of red-carpet celebrities with accompanying tips

Figure 8.3   Anticipated events

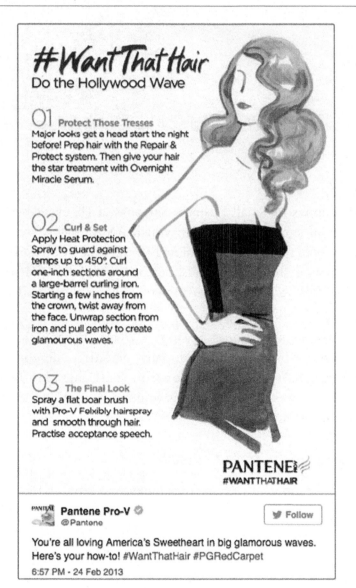

on how to achieve their hairstyles (Figure 8.3). Two years later, #WantThatHair even resurfaced as a trending topic during the 2015 Academy Awards.[9]

- Although Oreo's now-famous Super Bowl tweet captured the limelight, it was the fully staffed Super Bowl 'war room' (uniting all brand and agency stakeholders, as well as a legal team) that enabled the rapid design, approval, and publication of that tweet.[10]

- Turning our attention to another Super Bowl star... travel deals site Priceline released a series of short Vine videos that were essentially sped-up versions of existing Super Bowl ads. This garnered them favourable buzz amidst Super Bowl chatter and easily shareable content to disseminate – all without the hefty TV advertising price tag.[11]

Use case 3: location/object-based

A small but promising use case of RTM taps into location- and object-based triggers. A popular hand-crafted example of this type of RTM is when local food trucks publicize menus specials and their current location. Yet, increasingly sophisticated mobile near-field technologies, such as iBeacon, can target a consumer's location down to the store-shelf level and push a promotion to that person's phone at that moment. That is literally targeting the right person at the right time and the right place.

The emerging internet of things (IoT), where sensors are deployed throughout our physical world, creates dazzling possibilities for RTM to exist in true real time and with uncanny relevance. Marketers will have to understand how to balance expectations around engagement versus privacy, or face being seen as creepy. We will discuss how to make the most of contextual content and connected experiences in Chapter 11.

Some examples of the location/object-based use case include:

- Taco Bell partnered with GPS mapping app Waze to trigger location-based ads to appear on drivers' smartphones when they are near a restaurant – but safely and wisely, only when the car is stopped at a red light.[12]

- Macy's enables in-store targeting by installing Apple iBeacon transmitters throughout its flagship stores. Macy's then pushes special offers and recommendations to customers based on the specific department in range.[13]

- Van Leuween, a New York ice cream store, uses PayPal's app to detect customers' geolocation to entice them into nearby stores with discount offers and coupons (see Figure 8.4).[14] Customers are then allowed to pay for their sweet treats via PayPal.

- Whole Foods grocery chain partnered with Thinknear to place geofences around many stores (its own and competitors!) that would serve targeted ads and special discounts to passersby. The campaign resulted in a 4.69 per cent post-click conversion rate, more than three times the national average of 1.43 per cent.[15]

Use case 4: predictive analytics-based

Another relatively small but growing area of triggered RTM is based on predictive analytics. Amazon has been using predictive data for some time to display recommendations to customers based on browsing and purchase history. This practice is slowly being adopted by B2B marketers as well, sometimes combined with marketing automation solutions.

We predict the trend will gain momentum as data solutions become more accessible and simpler to implement:

- Salesforce.com uses its own tool set to track lead interactions with content (eg clicks, downloads, shares, time viewed, etc), funnelling this data back into its CRM and deploying automated follow-up content based on an individual leads phase in the purchasing process.[16]

- Hardware and software solutions provider CDW uses Lattice Engines data modelling and testing products to improve its marketing targeting across catalogues, direct mail and e-mail. By using predictive analytics to prioritize customers with higher likelihood to buy, CDW has been able to effectively raise response rates and average order value.[17]

Figure 8.4   Location/object-based

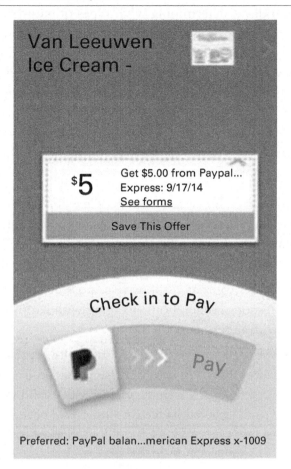

Van Leeuwen
Ice Cream -

$5   Get $5.00 from Paypal...
Express: 9/17/14
See forms

Save This Offer

Check in to Pay

Pay

Preferred: PayPal balan...merican Express x-1009

SOURCE Van Leeuwen Ice Cream

Use case 5: customer interaction

Customer interactions take many forms: CRM, customer service, handling complaints and community interactions being the primary examples. While many organizations handle such interactions within customer service, the very public, visible – and occasionally even viral – nature of these interactions in social channels means they are increasingly becoming the purview of the marketing organization.

This is especially true now that customers have come to expect brands to respond to their digital queries and complaints in near-real time.[18] This requires a combination of both reactive and anticipatory work: triage workflow, determining what types of messaging will be responded to and in which channels (public or private), empowering staff to address complaints, and having a breaking news communications plan ready for crises. It also means close coordination on all of the above between customer service, communications, and marketing.

With 56 per cent of companies utilizing RTM to form customer relationships,[19] this category can span many departments and roles. This includes traditional customer service, community building, crisis management and more:

- Pretzel Crisps listened for tweets from people who tweeted that they were hungry, but not sure what to eat. The company then replied back to them with an offer to send product samples.[20] In some cases, they even showed up at workplaces with a basket of snacks.

- JetBlue uses Twitter to be as responsive as possible (aiming for less than an hour response time), both engaging with happy customers and helping frustrated ones.

- smart USA responded to a particularly snarky tweet that claimed, 'Saw a bird had crapped on a Smart Car. Totalled it.' The brand responded by designing a hilarious, scientifically valid infographic (see Figure 8.5) and tweeted back, 'Couldn't have been one bird, @ adtothebone. Sounds more like 4.5 million. (Seriously, we did the maths).'[21]

Use case 6: breaking news

The most reactive form of RTM is responding in a legitimate, relevant manner to unanticipated breaking news. This can also be the most spontaneous, challenging and difficult type of RTM that brands will encounter. Advanced preparation is all but impossible, and all too often breaking news is not good news, so an acute degree of sensitivity is called for. The requirement is often not just getting a polished message out in a short period of time in reaction to an event, but also following the arc of a story as it unfolds. There is an opportunity in this use case to hit it over the fence by appropriately leveraging the event in a way that is contextually relevant, both to the event and to the brand.

Figure 8.5   Customer interaction

SOURCE SmartCar on Twitter

For example, Coca-Cola announced it was suspending all brand advertising dollars for a month and putting that spending into relief towards Typhoon Haiyan disaster recovery in the Philippines.[22] The company donated US \$2.5 million towards the cause and received significant global recognition, publicity and social amplification by leveraging real time to maximize the impact of the announcement (see Figure 8.6).

Figure 8.6 Coca-Cola mentions after announcing Typhoon Haiyan relief

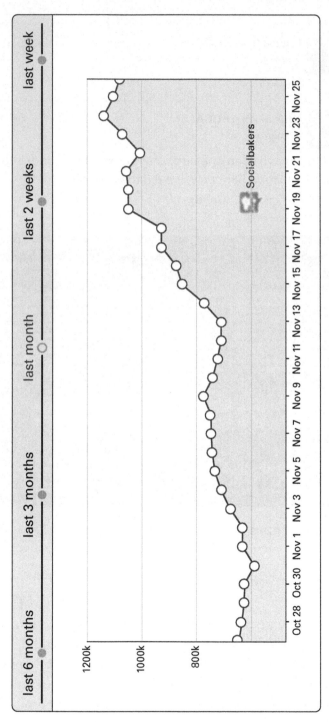

Coca-Cola People Talking About

SOURCE SocialBakers

Figure 8.7 KitKat 'Bendgate' tweet

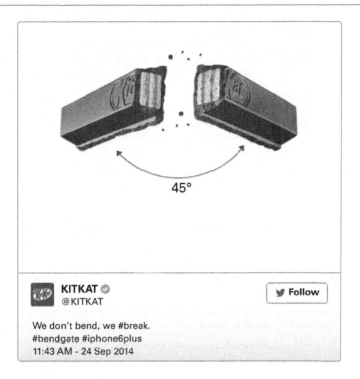

SOURCE Ad Week [Online] http://www.adweek.com/news/advertising-branding/how-kitkats-awesome-bendgate-tweet-came-together-30-minutes-160414

Nestlé took a lighter approach to other *breaking* news, poking fun at the pliability and related consumer complaints of the iPhone 6+ after it was released (see Figure 8.7). At the time of its publishing, a KITKAT® tweeted joke was the most retweeted brand post of all time (even beating out Oreo).[23]

Risks involved

An important risk to consider is inappropriate or insensitive posting around an event. This is when brands inject themselves into event commentary in a way that is artificial, overly promotional, irrelevant to the brand or just plain crass – often termed 'culture-jacking'. Epicurious found itself backpedalling and apologizing in the wake

Figure 8.8   Example of poorly executed real-time marketing

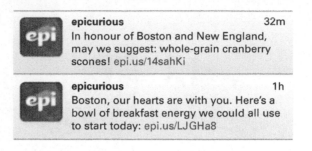

SOURCE Twitter

Figure 8.9   Netflix responds to cultural event with finesse and humour

SOURCE Twitter (2014)

of the Boston Marathon bombings when preloaded tweets promoting cranberry scones went live shortly after the tragedy. A real-time response expressing condolences, yet promoting another recipe, only fanned the flames (see Figure 8.8).

Adobe's Chad Warren sees this as: 'In a desperate effort to stay relevant, brands attach themselves to any and everything, losing sight of what their audiences actually care about and see in the brand.'

It can be done right, however, if a brand knows its audience and accurately judges the inferred levity of a potentially dicey situation. For example, when soccer star Luis Suarez bit an opponent during the World Cup, Netflix tweeted a connection between his actions and 'devouring' a season of *House of Cards*, a popular Netflix original series (see Figure 8.9).

Preparing for RTM requires two types of planning

How companies prepare for real time will dictate the effectiveness of RTM programmes. We found that planning falls into two areas, one that looks at the overall strategy and approach to RTM and the other that focuses on the organization and resources needed to execute RTM itself. Figure 8.10 outlines the top 12 steps that businesses should take to maximize success and scale in RTM (see Figure 8.10):

Planning strategy

This first phase of preparing lays a foundation of customer understanding, goals and content strategy that is essential.

Listen and learn

Success in real time is contingent on understanding your audience, who they are, where they go, what they care about, how they perceive the brand, etc. While traditional research methods such as focus groups and surveys are instructive towards this end, the literal real-time nature of RTM requires more real-time information gathering. Listening and analytics tools help monitor the audience's pulse, sentiments, behaviours and buzz, as it happens and as it evolves. Are customers complaining about not getting a response? What are competitors doing, and what is happening in adjacent industries?

Equally important is having the analytic capacity to mine findings from these discussions and apply learnings to continually improve campaigns and uncover new creative ideas and insights. Brands must always be listening and learning for cues from the audience, industry and pertinent cultural events – this is absolutely necessary to lay the foundation for being as relevant as possible with RTM.

Define RTM business goals

The next step to RTM preparedness is defining the goals that RTM will serve, both at a programme and business level, eg brand relevance, favourability, consideration, purchase intent, etc. Be sure to extend

Figure 8.10 12 steps to prepare for real-time marketing

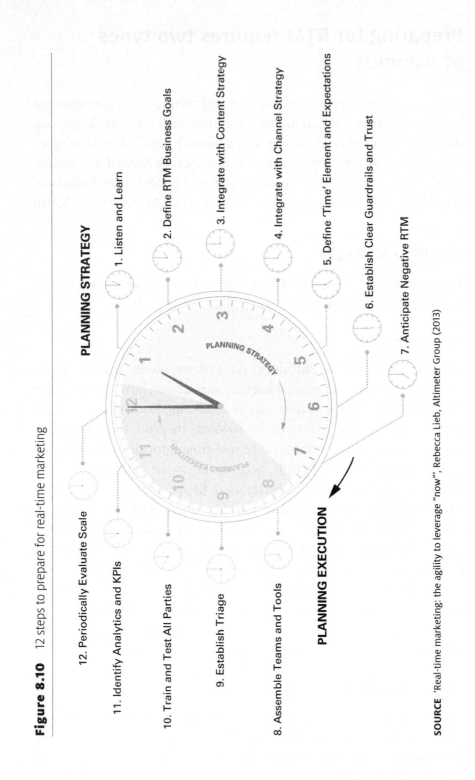

PLANNING STRATEGY

1. Listen and Learn
2. Define RTM Business Goals
3. Integrate with Content Strategy
4. Integrate with Channel Strategy
5. Define 'Time' Element and Expectations
6. Establish Clear Guardrails and Trust
7. Anticipate Negative RTM

PLANNING EXECUTION

8. Assemble Teams and Tools
9. Establish Triage
10. Train and Test All Parties
11. Identify Analytics and KPIs
12. Periodically Evaluate Scale

SOURCE 'Real-time marketing: the agility to leverage "now"', Rebecca Lieb, Altimeter Group (2013)

this beyond simply the number of times that a post gets favourited. Aligning real time with existing business goals is important, because it helps contextualize and justify the programme to executive decision makers and will increase the likelihood for executive sponsorship as the programme evolves across functions.

Integrate with content strategy

Aligning RTM with content strategy is foundational to creating guidelines around what, how and when to respond, publish and listen. Integrating real time into the greater content marketing strategy also provides a reference point for rapid decision making around brand relevance, messaging and strategy.

Content strategy should not only have guidelines around voice, tone, point of view, messaging, brand values, etc, but should also invest in educating those executing in real time, whether they are brand employees or agency partners. 'Develop a brand compass if you don't already have one, and apply it to real-time marketing', explains Sabrina Caluori, SVP of digital media and marketing at HBO. 'Set the boundaries around what makes sense for you to participate in and what doesn't, so that every time something is trending, the team isn't asking, "Is this appropriate?"'

At an executional level, integration with strategy also aids in the creation of more anticipatory locked and loaded content assets, which facilitate the appearance of real time to customers, but can be created, approved and queued for deployment well in advance. In fact, real time can be integrated entirely with ongoing content marketing initiatives through modular, repurposeable, or even evergreen content hubs.

Pepsi Pulse exemplifies embedding a real-time approach into its content strategy through an evergreen content hub. The site aggregates hot content (tweets, videos, photos – largely earned) from across the web in an effort to provide visitors with the most inspiring musical, entertainment, sports and other cultural moments based on social popularity (see Figure 8.11).

Figure 8.11 Pepsi Pulse rounds up the latest cultural moments by social popularity

SOURCE Pepsi Pulse http://www.pepsi.com/es-us/d

Integrate with channel strategy

The *where* of RTM is as critically important to its success as content strategy. Channel strategy is dependent on many factors, including in what channels the target audience is to be found; the channel(s) in which relevant conversations are occurring; and having or having the ability to quickly make content assets that are appropriate to the channel in question (eg photos, videos, text, animated gifs, etc). Currently, the most critical channels for RTM are Twitter, Facebook, Instagram, Tumblr, Reddit, Snapchat and, of course, e-mail. Secondary, but still important, are owned channels, such as the company website, YouTube channels, mobile app, etc. Channel selection is always dependent on a variety of factors, including content strategy, audience targeting and rapidly shifting media habits.

Multinational and even many national enterprises must also consider time-zone issues simultaneously with channel strategy, as we touched on in Chapter 7. Having a separate Facebook page for India v the United Kingdom, for example, or for the Northeast v the Southwestern United States, may be as much a component of RTM strategy as it is cultural relevance when it is important to generate conversation, excitement, buzz or other RTM initiatives around a local event, be it news or even local weather.

Define 'time' element and expectations

Not all organizations are prepared to operate 24/7 or to respond to customer queries with literal immediacy. The Clorox Company currently has a response goal of one hour or less as they consider ramping up to a 24/7 environment. Dell aligns its customer support around near-real time in their policy to respond to 100 per cent of inbound customer interactions within a two-hour time period, through the channel in which it was received.

Real time can also span a continuum of days, weeks and even months (eg the BP Gulf oil spill or the Icelandic volcano ash cloud). The temporal definition of (and imperative to respond in) real time depends on the context and will differ by situation, organization and business goal. Ultimately, brands must define what real time means for their unique programmes and channels – and then let this guide expectations for responding and publishing, based on organizational capabilities.

Establish clear guardrails and trust

Perhaps the biggest obstacle to the adoption of RTM is the perceived barrier of approval processes: internal, legal, client, etc. Yet the organizations that are practising RTM most successfully shrug off this concern. 'We have a great relationship with legal', is a typical, dismissive response to what, for others, is a seemingly insurmountable obstacle. We have unearthed the following best practices to predefine guardrails before operating in real time and then streamline processes once deployed:

- Simplify legal approval to a yes/no response. Standard legal approvals can take hours, days, even weeks. These are aeons in the world of real time, where every second can make the difference between crisis and diffusion. Sketching out potential scenarios in advance helps twofold: one, by streamlining the approval process when acting in real time; and two, by exposing legal to anticipated scenarios early on.

- Have the necessary teams on deck. Whether in the room or a phone call away, it is critical to have access to key stakeholders involved (or who may need to be involved) when deploying in real time. Common stakeholders include those responsible for creative, copywriting, the brand team, the social team, the measurement team, corporate communications/PR and legal. For more anticipatory use cases, brands like Adobe assemble these stakeholders for weekly meetings to discuss newsworthy events and RTM as related to strategy. For more immediate use cases, accessibility is imperative.

- Construct a mini playbook. These will look less like traditional procedural handbooks and more like a list of three or four questions to which all RTM decisions must be accountable. Symantec, for example, developed three questions that all employees must ask and answer before posting: 'Am I creating unneeded risk to the brand?' 'Could this impact the company or myself negatively?' 'Would I want my grandmother to read this?' This simple system helps build confidence and empower employees to act autonomously but on behalf of the brand.

For a planned real-time event, such as the Emmy awards, HBO's Sabrina Caluori informs internal stakeholders (management, legal, communications) about overall strategy and what her team will do and react to – and then develops guidelines. 'We know we need freedom to develop content on the fly, but we need to know the guardrails [and] if anything we need to be escalated. There are built-in parameters for the campaign.'

Anticipate negative RTM

Opening up an organization to real-time events, reactions and inter-actions increases the risk of backlash and social media crises. While preparedness and governance help mitigate these risks, companies must actively and proactively be ready for anything. When it comes to societal events, brands can generally choose if, or to what degree, they want to chime into the conversation. But, when negative brand events are unfolding in real time, there is an imperative to respond and message in real time.

When brands find themselves in a foot-in-mouth situation, as Mountain Dew did in 2013, one of the best ways to recover is to amplify the apology itself in real time. After receiving a tremendous backlash and accusations of racism and misogyny for its 'Felicia the Goat' video, Mountain Dew sponsored its own apology in the form of a promoted tweet, as shown in Figure 8.12.

Active preparation for negative RTM includes direct communica-tion with corporate communications/PR and legal; clear guidelines around what, how and where to respond and message; and a plan for action, apology or improvement. Prepare proactively for nega-tive RTM through monitoring social buzz with listening tools, setting alerts for suspect mentions or keywords, and staying agile.

Planning execution

Once you have your strategy in place, it is then time to turn to the execution side of RTM, and in particular enabling it to happen in a seamless, scalable way.

Figure 8.12   Mountain Dew promotes apology tweet after ad blunder

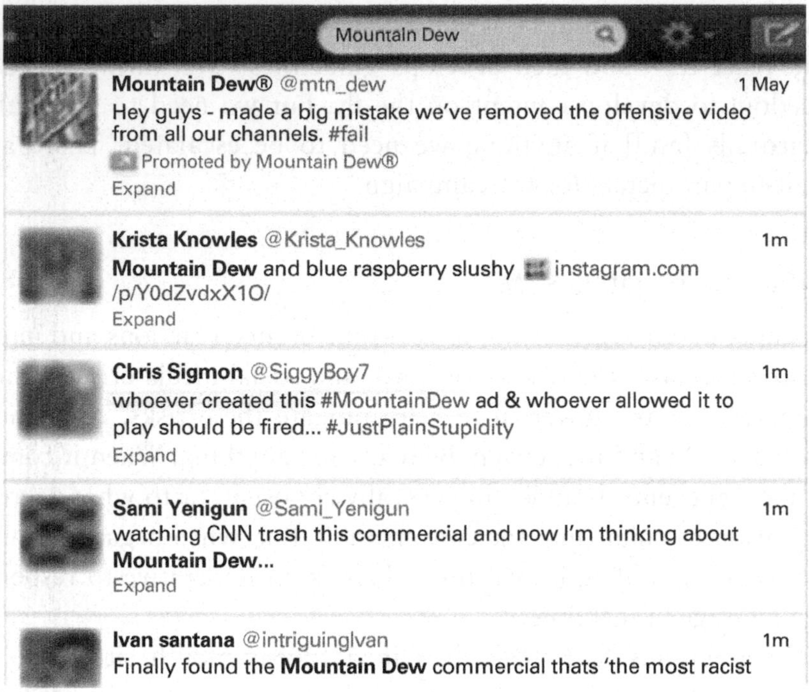

Assemble teams and tools

Successful RTM requires the right constituents be available, informed, educated and empowered. Assemble the proper teams (ie social, creative, copywriting, legal, PR, etc) and tools (ie listening, analytics, design, digital assets, publishing tools, etc.) to ensure streamlined execution. To this end, multiple companies we interviewed underscored the importance of having a 'war room', akin to a newsroom of sorts, where all teams can literally be present and collaborate together and in real time.

This can take three forms, depending on the use case that the team serves. For unplanned, reactive RTM execution, either the existing content hub or social media team takes the lead or a pre-identified and trained virtual team that has been identified in advance leaps into action. For anticipated events, a war room is often the hub, driving approvals, design, triage and publication in real time. Even brands without 24/7 RTM teams can assemble trained, prepared teams for special events, as Oreo did for the Super Bowl.

Anticipated or planned events with content created in advance assemble teams with regularly scheduled meetings to discuss event strategies and guidelines, as well as identify areas of opportunity. 'At Adobe', explains Chad Warren, 'we operate a creative newsroom that meets on a regular basis to identify upcoming items to plan (eg news, events, etc) and talk about what is relevant, what we could do more of, where we could take certain ideas. We have the right people in the room on an ongoing basis so that we don't need a lot of levels of approval and everyone understands their role – this helps us to go from ideation to action much more quickly.'

Establish triage

Establishing how to triage based on scenarios is one of the single most effective ways to streamline RTM execution. It reduces the need to be fully reactive by connecting certain cues or events that will trigger repeatable workflows.

For instance, community managers should be able to identify what types of language indicate threats or risks for the brand and how and when to escalate them to legal, PR or the appropriate team. When developing content for RTM, consider how users may respond, and then identify what warrants response and build workflows based on positive and negative interactions or needs. Consider all employees and teams involved, how team members will communicate, and how to handle messaging in a personalized and human way. The more detail provided, the more teams accounted for and the more scenarios planned for, the better.

Train and test all parties

A big part of operating in real time is enabling key employees to be and feel trusted and empowered to act on their judgement. This level of confidence is really only achieved through thorough education and training across all stakeholders – not only those posting and responding, but those creating, approving, distributing and monitoring, both internally and externally (ie agencies and vendors). Training should include both strategic and executional (tactical) elements:

- **Strategic training:**
  - How RTM is integrated with the larger content and brand strategies.
  - RTM's role across the organization (eg customer service, sales, HR, etc).
  - Deep training around the brand identity, voice, vision, risks, affiliations and programmes.
  - Which channels will support RTM, which will not, and why.
  - How the RTM programme will be measured and optimized.
  - The role of agencies and technology vendors (if applicable).
- **Executional training:**
  - Guidelines, guardrails, roles, triages, response-time requirements.
  - How to manage workflows based on RTM's role across the organization, as well as when triaging to other functions.
  - Sample scenarios of how customers, the crowd and media could respond to RTM.
  - How to leverage measurement and reporting to plan and act in real time.
  - Best practices using technologies supporting RTM.
  - Resources (eg contacts, phone numbers, vendor support, etc).
  - Training tools and testing will vary for each organization, based on resources and stakeholders. The goal of training and testing, however, is universal: to establish confidence for those executing, and trust in them, by all stakeholders, management and the brand at large.

Identify analytics and KPIs

As with any programme, you don't know where you are going unless you know where you are. RTM measurement instructs the effectiveness of current efforts, as well as pinpoint areas to explore more deeply. Listening should inform planning, targeting and action, as outlined above. Analytics capabilities monitor performance and optimization. Define KPIs for RTM by aligning them with overarching content strategy indicators. Real-time analytics capabilities are also important to RTM in order to capitalize on every effort made – not just the bigger, more planned initiatives, but the lesser planned, more reactive ones as well.

Finally, performance measurement of real-time engagement, content and activities should tie to support and help optimize the convergence of paid, owned and earned media. To this end, RTM can be an effective testbed for larger content initiatives; a support hub for triaging customers to owned properties or helpful content; or even provide clues or fodder for developing catchy ads and promotions. Measuring these efforts instructs where to invest time and resources across all brand assets.

Evaluate scale periodically

'But will it scale?' is a very real question in real time, particularly regarding staffing and customer channels. For large brands that have traffic and interactions numbering in the thousands per day, real time carries a host of risks that must be addressed when thinking about response at scale. Enterprises must frequently (eg monthly or quarterly) assess and evaluate the scale of their RTM initiatives: headcount, talent, tools, roles, etc.

Appropriately scaling RTM is complex, difficult and cost-intensive, necessitating frequent reviews and assessments against business goals. Scale must be evaluated on a foundation of benchmarking against KPIs. Adobe's Chad Warren explains, 'If you don't have a means to understand whether something is working in your favour or not, you will have trouble knowing when and where to scale those efforts.'

RTM is a present reality, not a distant future, for enterprises functioning in the digital age. The speed and immediacy of news cycles and social media, not to mention the very public media sphere in which brand and product events operate, make it imperative that enterprises strategically adopt RTM in a fashion that will both benefit the business now and scale to address future requirements.

Notes

1 Emarketer (2016) [accessed 6 January 2017] Emarketer Roundup: Real Time Marketing in the World of Data, *Emarketer* [Online] https://www.emarketer.com/public_media/docs/eMarketer_Roundup_ Real_Time_Marketing_World_Data.pdf

2 Campbell, C (2016) [accessed 6 January 2017] 52% of Customers Expect Your Brand to Respond to Their Reviews, *Socialmediatoday* [Online] http://www.socialmediatoday.com/ marketing/52-customers-expect-your-brand-respond-their-reviews

3 Golin Harris (2012) [accessed 6 January 2017] Four Reasons to Add Real-Time Marketing to Your Mix, *Golin Harris Research* [Online] http://golinharris.com/wp- content/uploads/2012/02/Insights_ RealTimeMarketing_ Downloadable-PDF3.pdf

4 Emarketer (2015) [accessed 6 January 2017] As Real-Time Marketing ROI Increases, Spending Follows, *Emarketer* [Online] http://www. emarketer.com/Article/Real-Time-Marketing-ROI-Increases-Spending- Follows/1012622#sthash.PhVJG5xR.dpuf

5 Emarketer (2016) [accessed 6 January 2017] Emarketer Roundup: Real Time Marketing in the World of Data, *Emarketer* [Online] https://www.emarketer.com/public_media/docs/eMarketer_Roundup_ Real_Time_Marketing_World_Data.pdf

6 Moth, D (2014) [accessed 6 January 2017] 10 Very Cool Examples of Experiential Marketing, *EConsultancy* [Online] https://econsultancy. com/blog/65230-10-very-cool-examples-of-experiential-marketing/

7 Cho, J (2016) [accessed 6 January 2017] Shop Small [Online] https:// www.americanexpress.com/us/small-business/shop-small/

8 Moth, D (2014) [accessed 6 January 2017] 10 Very Cool Examples of Experiential Marketing, *EConsultancy* [Online] https://econsultancy. com/blog/65230-10-very-cool-examples-of-experiential-marketing/

9 Narain, G (2015) [accessed 6 January 2017] Here's Why Real- Time Marketing Won't Work (And What Will), *Content Marketing Institute* [Online] http://contentmarketinginstitute.com/2015/04/ real-time-marketing-wont-work/

10 Edwards, J (2013) [accessed 6 January 2017] Oreo's Super Bowl Power-Outage Tweet was 18 Months in the Making, *Business Insider* [Online] http://www.businessinsider.com/oreos-super-bowl-power- outage-tweet-was-18-months-in-the-making-2013-3?IR=T

11 Klein, M (2015) [accessed 6 January 2017] Which Brands get Real-Time Right?, *Falcon* [Online] https://www.falcon.io/insights-hub/topics/content-marketing/examples-of-real-time-marketing/#GEN

12 Adweek (2012) [accessed 6 January 2017] Taco Bell's Digital Guacamole, *Adweek* [Online] http://www.adweek.com/news/technology/taco-bells-digital-guacamole-146149

13 Luncden, I (2013) [accessed 6 January 2017] Apple's iBeacon Comes to Retailers via Shokick's ShopBeacon, *TechCrunch* [Online] https://techcrunch.com/2013/11/20/shopkick-rolls-out-ibeacon-enabled-shopping-alerts-with-shopbeacon-with-macys-as-its-first-trialist/

14 Girish, D (2016) [accessed 6 January 2017] 4 Brands that are Winning at Location-Based Marketing and How, *Beaconstac* [Online] http://blog.beaconstac.com/2016/04/4-brands-that-are-winning-at-location-based-marketing-and how/

15 Girish, D (2016) [accessed 6 January 2017] 4 Brands that are Winning at Location-Based Marketing and How, *Beaconstac* [Online] http://blog.beaconstac.com/2016/04/4-brands-that-are-winning-at-location-based-marketing-and-how/

16 Salesforce (2013) [accessed 6 January 2017] Inside Salesforce.com's Social Media Strategy, *Slideshare* [Online] http://www.slideshare.net/Salesforce/inside-salesforcecoms-social-media-strategy

17 Lattice (2016) [accessed 6 January 2017] CDW Success Story: Driving Business Success with Predictive Analytics [Online] http://lattice-engines.com/blog/cdw-success-story-driving-business-success-with-predictive-analytics

18 Campbell, C (2016) [accessed 6 January 2017] 52% of Customers Expect Your Brand to Respond to Their Reviews, *Social Media Today* [Online] http://www.socialmediatoday.com/marketing/52-customers-expect-your-brand-respond-their-reviews

19 Emarketer (2016) [accessed 6 January 2017] Emarketer Roundup: Real-Time Marketing in the World of Data, *Emarketer* [Online] https://www.emarketer.com/public_media/docs/eMarketer_Roundup_Real_Time_Marketing_World_Data.pdf

20 Roberts, M (2012) [accessed 6 January 2017] Pretzel Crisps Uses Superbowl Social Media Buzz to Engage with Twitter Users, *MegRoberts.Wordpress* [Online] http://megroberts.wordpress.com/2012/02/10/pretzel-crisps-uses-super-bowl-social-media-buzz-to-engage-with- twitter-users/

21 Nudd, T (2013) [accessed 6 January 2017] 8 Types of Real-Time Marketing, and the Brands that Got It Right, *Adweek* [Online] http://www.adweek.com/news-gallery/advertising-branding/8-types-real-time-marketing-and-brands-got-it-right-152261#intro

22 The Coca-Cola Company (2013) [accessed 6 January 2017] Updated: Coca-Cola Contributes More Than US$2.5 Million in Typhoon Relief Aid, *Coca-Cola Journey* [Online] http://www.coca-colacompany.com/press-center/press-releases/coca-cola-contributes-more-than-us-25-million-in-typhoon-relief-aid

23 Adweek (2014) [accessed 6 January 2017] KitKat's #Bendgate Tweet Had Officially Eclipsed Oreo's Super Bowl Win, *Adweek* [Online] http://www.adweek.com/news/advertising-branding/how-kitkats-awesome-bendgate-tweet-came-together-30-minutes-160414 (*KITKAT* is a registered trademark of Société des Produits Nestlé SA, Vevey, Switzerland)

Content marketing software 09

The content marketing tool landscape is crowded, rapidly changing and highly inconsistent. Marketers struggle to select the right tools not only for their own content marketing needs, but also solutions that integrate with enterprise, process and platform concerns. This chapter helps marketers to make informed buying choices by mapping eight needs scenarios to the existing vendor landscape.

Why content marketing tool selection is so difficult

It used to be so simple. Content marketing consisted merely of writing content and putting it on a website. It has now evolved into a complex process involving multiple players throughout the organization, outside agencies and vendors, multimedia and a proliferation of channels. Growing channel and media complexity, as well as increasing adoption of content marketing, has given rise to a large, complex and highly disparate content marketing software landscape.

Understanding what tools are available and, more importantly, what tools are needed for content marketing efforts, echoes the proverb of the blind men describing an elephant. There are point systems, enterprise solutions and hybrids, yielding very few apples-to-apples comparisons in the marketplace.

Complicating an already complicated set of choices is the fact that marketers still have a scattershot approach to content. Research shows that only 44 per cent of marketers consider their content strategies at least 'moderately effective'.[1] Despite a growing awareness (and acceptance) of the fact that content is the atomic particle of all marketing – essential for fuelling paid, owned and earned media – organizations lack a cohesive, coherent, strategic approach to content.

Other trends driving the complexity of the content marketing tools decision include the following:

- Content creation pressure: creating and publishing content is hard, unrelenting work. As a result, marketers tend to focus on the tactics of creation and just 'getting content done'. Exacerbating this is a campaign focus – if content strategy exists at all, it typically revolves around individual campaigns.

- Lack of strategy begets tool proliferation: ad hoc execution without goals, processes, communication and governance inevitably leads to ad hoc tools and random platform purchasing. The result is overlapping workflows and a hotchpotch of tools that are fragmented and often redundant.

- Lack of enterprise integration: when solutions are acquired haphazardly, they often do not integrate or work with other enterprise systems. Few marketers integrate their content tools and processes such as inbound marketing platforms, business intelligence or CRM. Yet when pressed, the same marketers have long lists of needed integrations from their content systems. Beyond technology platform integration, digital content workflows also exist, mainly on their own, with little integration into organizational processes.

- Misaligned buyer needs versus planned investments: our 2014 survey found that 67 per cent of marketers state audience identification and targeting as a top need – pointing to the trend of content aligning with advertising and other marketing initiatives. Yet, only 25 per cent are actively investing in this area (see Figure 9.1). The need to scale-up content creation is a tactical distraction from deeper strategic needs. Interestingly, our research found that vendor investment in product improvements correlate and align with marketers' stated needs rather than their planned investments.

Figure 9.1 depicts needs and investments across the eight primary content marketing use cases. In this chapter, we assess marketer needs and vendor solutions through the lens of these eight use cases, in order to facilitate proper alignment between the two.

Figure 9.1 Buyers' needs don't match planned investments

Base: Altimeter Group Content Marketing Survey 2014, n = 80 marketers

SOURCE 'The content marketing software landscape', Rebecca Lieb, Altimeter Group (2014)

A tangled vendor landscape complicates the picture

Because content marketing has so many permutations across hundreds of platforms, the content marketing tool's landscape is a mishmash of vendors, categories and technology platforms that make it difficult, if not impossible, to make apples-to-apples comparisons between solutions. While some basic technology maps of content marketing tools exist, they support neither vendors' go-to-market strategy nor marketers' decision-making processes.[2] Making this even more confusing are three trends, as set out below.

Trend 1: many solutions exist

Tools to manage, create, measure, optimize and otherwise wrangle content marketing are rapidly proliferating. We have identified more than 110 content marketing vendors, exclusive of certain categories, including e-mail, marketing automation, content management systems (CMSs), digital asset management solutions (DAMs) and social media management software (SMMS). The market is diverse and multifaceted. Mergers and acquisitions (M&A) activity is rapid. Just tracking the content vendor ecosystem is a near full-time job.

Trend 2: the content vendor landscape is sharply bifurcated

The majority is small – only 6 per cent of companies we examined have more than 100 employees and are not yet profitable. One-third offer a freemium model within which one-third of their customers pay nothing for the service. Of course, a small handful of giants – namely, Adobe, Oracle and Salesforce.com – loom over the landscape, all rapidly acquiring and consolidating players. These giants serve the entire marketing spectrum, brand themselves as 'marketing clouds', and are beginning to use terms such as 'content alignment' and 'converged media' in sales collateral and value propositions.

Trend 3: content marketing evolution is driving consolidation

We found that the movement of content marketing towards converged media – organizations are developing capabilities to make owned content more fluid so it can be used, optimized and deployed in shared (usually social media) and paid (advertising) channels – creates pressure for vendors to match this emerging need with fuller offerings.

As we presented in Chapter 3, Figure 9.2 illustrates the relationship between converged media and content marketing use cases, which are often transmedia in nature. This convergence of media development and deployment is contributing to the evolution of the content 'stack', away from disparate point solutions serving limited needs.

In some cases, point solutions are being strung end-to-end to create increasingly broader content marketing platforms. For example, Scripted, Percolate and Contently, which all began as written-word providers, have since added graphics capabilities into their tool sets.

The giant providers are also jumping in. Recent major moves include Adobe's purchase of content marketing specialist Livefyre; Oracle's acquisition of Eloqua, Responsys and Compendium; and Salesforce.com snapping up ExactTarget, Buddy Media and Pardot. IBM also made a foray into the space by buying Silverpop.

Figure 9.2 Media convergence drives content-stack evolution

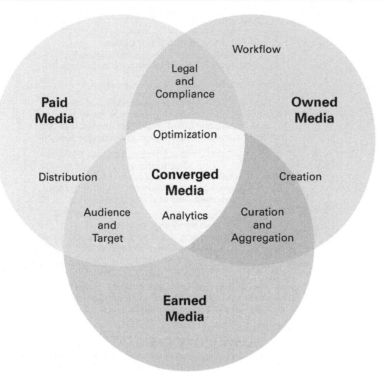

SOURCE 'The content marketing software landscape', Rebecca Lieb, Altimeter Group (2014)

Content stacks will emerge

While fragmented today, we believe that the content marketing tool landscape will begin to consolidate in earnest. In coming years, there will be 'content stack' offerings in the marketplace – end-to-end solutions akin to ad stacks (see Figure 9.3). Currently, no single vendor has an end-to-end solution. Eventually, a few will partner, merge, acquire and/or collaborate to create a total solution.

Content solutions will also soon absorb other software categories. For example, the distinction between SMMSs and content marketing tools is blurring and will soon vanish, as marketers and vendors demand content capabilities in a growing number of platforms. This will render most social-only tools redundant.

Figure 9.3   Content tool-stack hierarchy

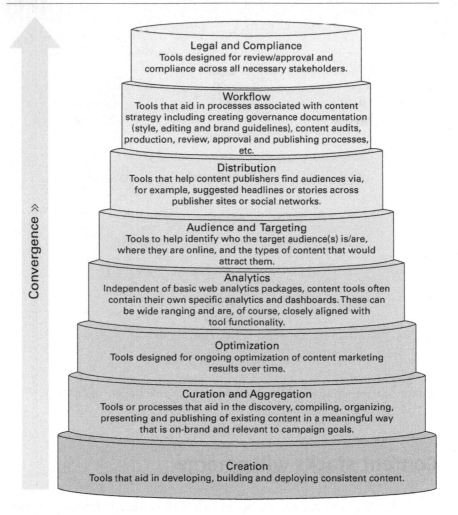

SOURCE 'The content marketing software landscape', Rebecca Lieb, Altimeter Group (2014)

Technology decisions must begin with use cases

We approach the content marketing tools problem from the perspective of marketing challenges and needs first, asking what challenges face content marketers today and how can technology help solve them. As marketer needs evolve over time, so will solutions sets. The key is not more or better point solutions but how they come together. That's why we recommend taking the following three steps to determine your content marketing tool stack:

- Determine your content marketing use cases.
- Plan for integration and evolution.
- Identify and prioritize vendors based on those use cases.

Step 1: determine content marketing use cases

We have identified three content marketing scenarios, laddering up from an immature 'feed-the-beast' tactical approach to a mature, process-driven, strategic stage (see Figure 9.4). Throughout these scenarios, we found eight overarching content marketing use cases, each with a complement of sub-categories. The eight use cases fall into roughly three phases – feed the beast, refine, govern – and escalate in complexity.

Feed the beast

In this initial phase, the organization struggles to keep up with the unrelenting demands of regularly creating quality content for one or more channels. They typically lack a coherent strategy and have only a bare-bones organizational structure (often stemming out of social media). They require a steady stream of ideas and inspiration, as well as the basic tools of content creation. Ultimately, this phase is characterized by the need to master the foundational use cases in content marketing: efficiently creating and collecting content at scale.

Refine

In this scenario, process is applied to content creation and production. This is the stage at which a team begins to take shape and roles

Figure 9.4 Three content marketing scenarios drive tool selection

SOURCE 'The content marketing software landscape', Rebecca Lieb, Altimeter Group (2014)

beyond content creation form, eg analytics. Content is audited and assessed, often with a formal scoring or grading process. Channels, audience and persona considerations play a greatly expanded role in creation. Content is optimized for digital and social distribution, and efforts are made to identify repeatable, sustainable content practices. The leader of the content group makes a more concerted effort to connect content development with the broader marketing teams. The refinement phase in content marketing is about getting smarter, optimizing processes, insights, targeting and programme deployment.

Govern

In this scenario, there is a need for the content strategy to be formalized and communicated throughout the enterprise; for example, governance and processes are firmly established to meet regulatory requirements. Focus shifts towards expanding the team and its ability to create experiential, engaging, multimedia content rather than simpler stories and informational pieces. Content is created with a view towards being reusable and/or repurposed across paid and earned, as well as owned, media channels. Legal and industry compliance rules and regulations are understood, and guardrails are in place to ensure compliance.

To help identify use cases, take a look at the more granular subcategories within each use case (Figure 9.5) and assess those needs that apply to your organization. As a best practice, also be certain to solicit stakeholders and end users for requirements, input and collaboration.

Step 2: plan for integration and evolution

Integration considerations are essential because of the pending consolidation driven by converged media, as well as the evolution of content stacks. Each of the eight content marketing use cases come with a host of potential integration issues, yet only 10 per cent of marketers say their content marketing technologies are 'fully integrated across people, processes and platforms'.[3] Identifying essential integrations can help refine a final list of prospective vendors.

Content marketing software integration is tripartite:

Figure 9.5 Content marketing use cases

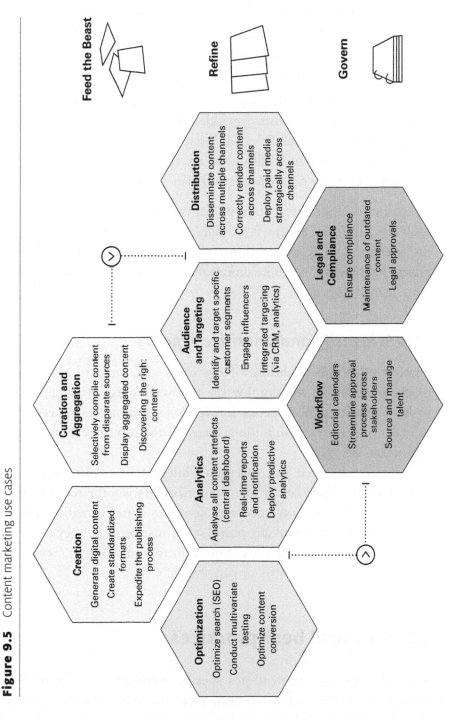

SOURCE 'The content marketing software landscape', Rebecca Lieb, Altimeter Group (2014)

- Integration with systems: this includes legacy and often future platforms such as data and analytics, CRM and inbound marketing.

- Integration with the organization such as internal communications, corporate intelligence and internal networks.

- Integration with processes, including workflow and organizational structure. This may include taking outside partners and/or agencies into account. 'You can't retrofit activities to the tool; you have to align the tool with your activities', according to Kristina Halvorson, CEO and founder of Brain Traffic.

There are common integration points that marketers leverage across each use case (see Figure 9.6). While not universal to all marketers' scenarios, these integrations fall into eight primary categories. Figure 9.6 charts how these common points of integration typically map against use cases.

Step 3: identify and prioritize vendors

Once a solid understanding of use cases and integration needs is reached, marketers can employ the following checklist (Figure 9.7) to help prioritize those needs for vendor selection. Rank use cases in order of priority, maintaining focus on the top three to five most important use cases.

Having prioritized use cases and integration requirements, the next step is to figure out which vendors can satisfy the requirements of those use cases. You may also consider working with multiple small vendors who provide point solutions, because they concentrate on key use cases that are important to your content marketing organization.

Content tool best practices

Regardless of an organization's specific software needs or level of content marketing sophistication, there are best practices around assessing, buying and introducing new content marketing software that are universally applicable.

Figure 9.6 Content Marketing Integration Needs

	Ad Exchange	Data and Analytics	Digital Media	Marketing Cloud	Search Engines	Sharing Platforms	Storage Platforms	Syndication Tools
	Display Inventory Sources Mobile Ad Servers Desktop Ad Servers	Web Analytics Business Intelligence CRM Mobile Data E-Commerce Platforms A/B Testing Tools	Publisher/News Outlets Blogs Video Platforms Audio Platforms Image Platform	Other CM Tools Marketing Automation SMMS Publishing and Embedding Tools E-mail Marketing Tools Influencer ID Tools	Search Engine Optimization	Social Networks Community Platforms Enterprise Collaboration Tools	Cloud Storage CMS DAM Web Server	RSS Feeds Syndication Widgets
Creation		x	x	x		x	x	
Curation and Aggregation			x	x	x	x	x	x
Optimization	x	x		x	x	x	x	
Audience and Target	x	x		x		x	x	
Analytics		x		x		x	x	
Distribution	x	x	x	x	x	x	x	x
Workflow				x		x	x	
Legal and Compliance	x		x	x				x

SOURCE 'The content marketing software landscape', Rebecca Lieb, Altimeter Group (2014)

Figure 9.7   Content marketing needs checklist

Marketer Needs	Use Case	Priority Integration(s)
☐ Generate digital content ☐ Create standardized content formats ☐ Expedite the publishing process	Creation	☐ Sharing Platforms ☐ Data and Analytics ☐ Digital Media ☐ Marketing Cloud ☐ Storage Platforms
☐ Compile content from disparate source ☐ Display aggregated content ☐ Discover the right content (for ideas, for sharing)	Curation and Aggregation	☐ Sharing Platforms ☐ Search ☐ Digital Media ☐ Marketing Cloud ☐ Storage Platforms ☐ Syndication Platforms
☐ Optimize search (SEO) ☐ Conduct multivariate testing ☐ Optimize content conversion	Optimization	☐ Sharing Platforms ☐ Ad Exchanges ☐ Search ☐ Data and Analytics ☐ Marketing Cloud ☐ Storage Platforms
☐ Identify and target specific customer segments ☐ Engage influencers ☐ Integrated targeting (via CRM, e-mail marketing, analytics, etc)	Audience and Targeting	☐ Sharing Platforms ☐ Ad Exchanges ☐ Data and Analytics ☐ Marketing Cloud ☐ Storage Platforms
☐ Analyse all content artefacts (central dashboard) ☐ Real-time reporting and notification ☐ Deploy predictive analytics to drive content marketing	Analytics	☐ Sharing Platforms ☐ Data and Analytics ☐ Marketing Cloud ☐ Storage Platforms

☐ Disseminate content across multiple channels
☐ Display content correctly across channels (incl.
  device types)
☐ Deploy paid media strategically across
  channels
	Distribution	☐ Sharing Platforms
		☐ Ad Exchanges
		☐ Search
		☐ Data and Analytics
		☐ Digital Media
		☐ Marketing Cloud
		☐ Storage Platforms
		☐ Syndication Platforms

☐ Organize content cadence ☐ Streamline approval process across necessary stakeholders ☐ Talent sourcing and management	Workflow	☐ Sharing Platforms ☐ Marketing Cloud ☐ Storage Platforms
☐ Profile content for compliance ☐ Store and disposal of historical content ☐ Legal approvals	Legal and Compliance	☐ Ad Exchanges ☐ Digital Media ☐ Marketing Cloud ☐ Syndication Platforms

SOURCE 'The content marketing software landscape', Rebecca Lieb, Altimeter Group (2014)

Train staff to use tools

And, train them on content marketing/strategy in general. Only 24 per cent of marketers say that employees are formally trained and empowered to publish on behalf of the brand.[4]

Avoid redundancies

There is considerable overlap in content marketing software functionality, eg, nearly all tools have some sort of built-in analytics dashboard. Yet, marketers often invest in a tool for its primary feature without realizing that there are secondary or tertiary features that they then buy elsewhere. Related to this is integration driving 'one version of the truth' versus 'multiple realities that don't align when viewed in aggregate'. This is an important consideration for cost efficiencies as well: 40 per cent of content marketers report that the lack of interdepartmental coordination is leading to disparate tools being used.[5]

Build for speed

How quickly and efficiently teams can implement, set up, train and use new tools is paramount, as is how quickly tools can 'deliver relevant content in a timely fashion', as Andrew Milburn, director of global channel product management at American Express, puts it. Foremost among marketers' planned investment in content marketing software are tools to aid in the rapid creation and deployment of content, particularly for those utilizing various forms of real-time marketing, as we covered in Chapter 8. Rapid personalization, delivery and the ability to build content based on buzz is a primary consideration.

Consider IT support (or lack thereof)

Whether a solution requires initial or ongoing support from IT is a consideration for many marketing organizations, particularly with an ever-increasing 'need for speed'. A growing trend is solutions that enable marketing to bypass IT for day-to-day publishing needs on owned media, such as design changes to a website.

Scale towards the future

Channels and tactics that marketers may not be using today – eg mobile, real-time marketing, native advertising, future enterprise technology investments, or localization for international markets – can rapidly become urgent realities that will require urgent integration. 'Can it scale?' is a difficult, yet essential, question when considering content marketing software investments. Internationalization and localization are often overlooked when global enterprises invest in tools. Language, local channels and platforms, and other region/country-specific considerations can be critical criteria.

Notes

1 O'Brien, M (2015) [accessed 6 January 2017] Only 2% of Marketers Have 'Very Effective' Content Strategy (Study), *Click Z* [Online] https://www.clickz.com/only-2-of-marketers-have-very-effective-content-strategy-study/25059/

2 For example, the Content LUMAscape, which can be found at Kawaja, T (2014) [accessed 6 January 2017] Content Marketing/Native LUMA scape [Online] http://www.slideshare.net/tkawaja/content-marketing-31091520

3 Lieb, R (2016) [accessed 6 January 2017] The Content Marketing Software Landscape: Research from Altimeter, a Prophet Company, *Altimeter* [Online] http://www2.prophet.com/content-marketing-software-landscape

4 Lieb, R (2016) [accessed 6 January 2017] The Content Marketing Software Landscape: Research from Altimeter, a Prophet Company, *Altimeter* [Online] http://www2.prophet.com/content-marketing-software-landscape

5 Lieb, R (2014) [accessed 6 January 2017] The Content Marketing Software Landscape: Marketer Needs and Vendor Solutions, *SlideShare* [Online] http://www.slideshare.net/lieblink/the-content-marketing-software-landscape-marketer-needs-vendor-solutions

Content marketing performance

10

While content marketing is pervasive, most organizations' ability to effectively measure their efforts fall significantly behind their ability to publish content to every screen. A 2016 study from Rapt Media shows that 59 per cent of strategists are most concerned with 'gaining deeper insights' when investing in content, and 98 per cent say they would invest more in content marketing software if it addressed this measurement concern.[1]

In addition to feeling hampered by their ability to measure content marketing effectiveness, marketers also measure too narrowly. New tools, channels and media platforms create new (and more complex) measurement opportunities, coupled with the fact that content marketing can be applied to a wide variety of revenue-related goals other than (or in addition to) sales. Measuring only for sales and leads – or simply relying on volume or vanity metrics such as 'likes' and 'views' that contain little business value – undermines and devalues investments in time, media, employees, technology and vendor relationships.

Moreover, as participation in content initiatives increases and permeates the outward-facing and non-marketing divisions such as human resources, customer service and support, product groups, R&D, etc, metrics and KPIs that are applied to content correspondingly shift. These divisions do not directly support sales but instead have their own unique success criteria. To encourage participation in content initiatives, these groups can only be incentivized if content marketing supports their individual and departmental goals that, clearly, are of high value to the organization. Demonstrating this value can only occur through measurement.

Applying meaningful metrics and KPIs will demonstrate value, help garner additional resources and investment, recruit support and participation in content initiatives, aid in optimizing campaigns, and enhance the understanding of consumer wants and needs. This drives organizational efficiency in content creation, production, publishing and dissemination across paid, owned and earned media alike.

A framework for content measurement

Beyond marketing and sales, content can play a critical role in improving brand health, augmenting the customer experience, reducing cost and risk, and many other goals of the business. Figure 10.1 illustrates the key value propositions of a well-crafted content strategy.

Figure 10.1   The business value of content strategy

Innovation
Collaborating with
customers to drive future
products and services

Brand Health
A measure of attitudes,
conversation and behaviour
towards your brand

Customer Experience
Improving your relationship
with customers, and their
experience with your brand

BUSINESS GOAL

Marketing Optimization
Improving the effectiveness
of marketing programmes

Operational Efficiency
Where and how your
company reduces expenses

Revenue Generation
Where and how your
company generates revenue

SOURCE 'Content marketing performance: a framework to measure real business impact', Rebecca Lieb and Susan Etlinger, Altimeter Group (2015)

Each point in the compass represents an opportunity for business-centric measurement; that is, measurement that directly ties to business objectives and strategies. For example, brand health metrics must actually quantify – in meaningful ways – the health of the brand, the drivers affecting that health and the changes over time. Operational efficiency metrics may refer to cost savings, risk, crisis management, or even productivity improvements.

Please note that organizational measurement strategies tend to be proprietary; companies typically do not want to share the 'secret sauce' that helps them to calibrate their content marketing and, by extension, business strategies. As a result, we have supplemented each case example in this chapter with an additional set of metrics to consider, as well as a rationale for using them.

These are meant to provide a starting point for organizations eager to derive deeper insights from the performance of their content. In many cases, the same 'raw' metrics can be used as ingredients to answer many types of questions. In other cases, there are business or strategy-specific metrics that require data from other tools or sources, such as web analytics, business intelligence, market research, e-mail marketing or CRM systems.

Brand health

Brand health is a measure of attitudes, conversations and behaviours directed towards the brand. It can be expressed in sentiment, topic drivers, sharing behaviour, likes, retweets and other measures of interest and attitude. While listening is a useful tactic to understand drivers of brand health, content can be useful to address issues, raise awareness and, overall, communicate at scale. From there, responses to content – viewing behaviour, sharing behaviour, sentiment expressed about the content, even audience growth – show how the content is performing and whether it is augmenting or detracting from the health of the brand.

CASE EXAMPLE

Seattle Seahawks

The problem
The Seattle Seahawks' social media team wanted to leverage the tremendous real-life conversations about the Seattle Seahawks authentically, but in a digital context. Its goal was to use the digital medium to build more engagement between the Seahawks and fans, rather than as an extension of broadcast.[2]

The approach
To increase engagement and better understand fan sentiment, the Seahawks' social media team used Simply Measured to assess content performance to determine which content resonated with fans, both as a community and as individuals (see Figure 10.2, Table 10.1 and Table 10.2; see also Figure 10.7 later in this chapter).

The result
The results of the Seahawks' social media efforts were clear: a 40 per cent increase in overall audience, measured by followers per platform, and a 173 per cent increase in engagement across social networks, measured as an aggregate of major channels (Facebook, Twitter, Instagram) and compared to an average during the playoffs. The Seahawks' social media team used this data to inform its communications strategies and measure and optimize its tactics going forward.

Figure 10.2   Dashboard for Seattle Seahawks' social media channels

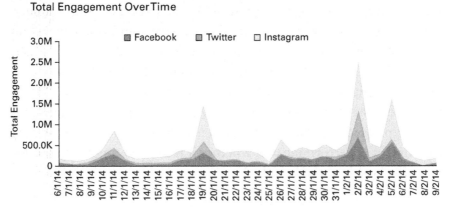

Total Engagement Over Time

SOURCE Simply Measured

Table 10.1 Core metrics used

Metric	What it can show
Engagement	Level of interest in the brand across multiple social and digital platforms
Audience Growth	Overall awareness and/or engagement; which platforms are most effective at reaching fans, which content resonates best, per platform

SOURCE 'Content marketing performance: a framework to measure real business impact', Rebecca Lieb and Susan Etlinger, Altimeter Group (2015)

Table 10.2 Other metrics to consider

Category	Metric	What it can show
Sentiment	Sentiment over time. Sentiment by channel. Sentiment by organization or competitor. Source of positive, negative and neutral sentiment. Top keywords. Day-parting analysis by conversation topic. Accelerating keywords, volume, sentiment	How your digital audience feels about you, how different channels (Facebook, web, Twitter, etc.) differ in terms of audience sentiment and concerns, what topics are resonating and why, during what time of day/week/month certain conversations occur, which conversations are picking up steam, and which are dying down

All of this can be used to inform marketing and future social strategies |
| Content Performance | Highest-performing topics, brands, regions, by content unit

Number of fans/followers, brand mentions by content unit. Top shared, liked, RTed, pinned, favourited, etc | Which topics, brands, platforms are most successful in terms of content engagement, sentiment audience acquisition, sharing behaviour. These metrics should be used as inputs to future content strategy and decision making |

(Continued)

Table 10.2   *(Continued)*

Category	Metric	What it can show
Share of Voice	Social Share of Voice (SSOV) over time vs. competitors'. Share of total conversation by industry, product, topic, content unit	While this is an imperfect metric (based on the intense volatility of the web), it can help to establish a baseline for several key indicators: how the brand's voice resonates overall, compared to those of competitors, within an industry or topic discussion, etc. Analysts should be sure to account for other external factors (product launches, holidays, major news cycles) that can affect results
Influencers	Influencers by topic (by followers and/or reach) Sentiment by influencer	Who among a brand's community is driving conversation and, potentially, influencing sentiment. Note that measuring the business impact of the influencer requires attribution of their content to a business outcome, but for brand health the key is to know who the advocates are, who the detractors are, and why

SOURCE 'Content marketing performance: a framework to measure real business impact', Rebecca Lieb and Susan Etlinger, Altimeter Group (2015)

Marketing optimization

This is an umbrella term encompassing the many components that can improve existing marketing efforts and take them to the next level.

CASE EXAMPLE

Rokenbok's YouTube page

The problem

Rokenbok manufactures high-end toys that combine construction sets with robotics. About five years ago, 80 per cent of the company's customers discovered the products in brick-and-mortar specialty toy stores, 20 per cent via word of mouth. There was no digital component to either sales or marketing. When economic shifts led to the decline of the specialty toy retailers that Rokenbok relied on to showcase and demonstrate its complex products, the company found itself threatened. 'It's not obvious to folks from static images what our toy system is, or how you play with it', says Rokenbok CEO Paul Eichen (see Figure 10.3).[3]

The approach

After experimenting with demos at malls and tradeshows, the company began to create mini-videos showcasing Rokenbok's toys. These serve not only to entertain, but also to demonstrate products that require a $50–$100 investment from buyers. The company does not expect a conversion at first touch, so relationship building is key. The company also showcases user-made videos on its YouTube channel, many made by teens who have been using the products

Figure 10.3   Rokenbok's YouTube page

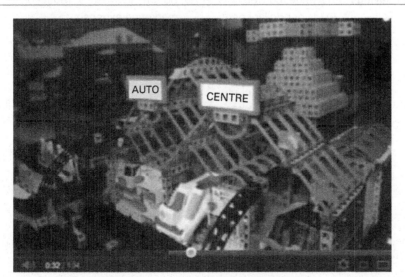

SOURCE Rokenbok/YouTube https://www.youtube.com/user/Rokenbok

since early childhood, creating retention, loyalty and word of mouth. Videos are also targeted to prospects with YouTube's TrueView in-stream and display ads, helping the company to discover target audiences and keywords relevant to their core kid and family segments.

The result

Half of Rokenbok's customers now come from YouTube, the number one source of traffic to the site. The company has transformed into an e-commerce-only business, from a very recent legacy of selling exclusively in bricks-and-mortar specialty stores. In short, Rokenbok's business model transformed via a goal-oriented content strategy.

Table 10.3   Core metrics used

Metric	What it can show
Referrers	Where traffic is coming from; which platforms generate the most referral traffic
E-mail sign-ups	Willingness to be contacted/marketed to (conversion)
Dwell time on site	Level of interest in the content

SOURCE 'Content marketing performance: a framework to measure real business impact', Rebecca Lieb and Susan Etlinger, Altimeter Group (2015)

Table 10.4   Other metrics to consider

Category	Metric	What it can show
Cost savings	Revenue, conversions, leads per dollar spent compared to traditional programmes	Bottom-line results: reduction in marketing expense Top-line results: revenue per dollar spent
	Revenue, conversions, leads by content unit	Lead sources: which content is most effective at generating leads
	Revenue, conversions, leads by channel	Lead sources: which platforms are most effective at generating leads
	Visit loyalty by content Visit loyalty by views/click-through for each channel	Which content provokes the most return visitors Which channels are most effective in terms of return visits and engagement

(Continued)

Table 10.4 *(Continued)*

Category	Metric	What it can show
	Sentiment, retweets, likes, fans, followers, pins by content unit	Most liked, popular, shared content (by post and by channel)
	Sentiment by channel	How time of day/week/month/year may affect content performance
	Retweets, likes, fans, followers by channel	
	Day-parting analysis by content unit	
	Sentiment by influencer	Which influencers are advocates, which are detractors. Which have the most influence by channel or topic
	Most active/followed by campaign, channel, content unit	

SOURCE 'Content marketing performance: a framework to measure real business impact', Rebecca Lieb and Susan Etlinger, Altimeter Group (2015)

Revenue generation

One of the knottiest challenges for content marketers is the ability – or lack thereof – to measure the impact of content on revenue generation. The major challenges of measurement are:

1 Content proliferates across multiple apps and browsers, fragmenting data capture. Tracking code does not always persist across browsers or applications, which makes it hard to track performance in aggregate.

2 Inability to capture consistent data. Some social networking apps either do not offer application program interfaces (APIs) or analytics, or frequently change APIs, which can degrade the ability to capture performance data.

3 Other methods can be helpful, but problematic. Correlations and A/B testing can sometimes yield insight into the impact of content on revenue, but the confidence levels of these methods is lower than direct measurement and depends on the availability of trained analysts who can properly craft the experiments and interpret the results.

4 Last-touch attribution does not capture the impact of content on high-consideration items or long-term sales cycles. As a result, sites such as Pinterest or Houzz, which act as sites for inspiration and aspiration, may be unfairly disadvantaged.

Following are examples of B2C brands that have been successful in overcoming the challenges of revenue attribution of their content.

Note: For context, B2B brands typically use metrics such as white-paper downloads, click to chat, contact me/e-mail me buttons and e-mail opt-in as proxies for or actual conversion metrics. They may also use A/B testing (percentage of people who have engaged with content who accept a meeting versus the percentage of those who have not) to gauge the impact of content on the buying decision. With the latter metric it is not always possible to determine a causal relationship. Did the content drive conversion, or do the people most likely to convert tend to be the biggest content consumers?

CASE EXAMPLE

Zenni Optical

The problem
Zenni Optical, a provider of prescription glasses and accessories, wanted to build brand awareness and drive sales, while increasing the efficiency of their marketing campaigns (Figure 10.4).[4]

The approach
Working with Wpromote, Zenni added a content layer to the customer journey and buying process, with the aim of making the experience of buying eyeglasses in the digital realm as fun and engaging as it can be offline. And, because the glasses are inexpensive, consumers have the option to treat their eyeglasses like accessories, and change them according to outfit or mood.[5]

The company used search and off-site content to drive new customer acquisition, incorporating leveraged e-mail marketing and social media such as Instagram hashtag campaigns (#zennifashion), blog posts and other tactics to support customers throughout the digital buying cycle. The idea was to use content to show how fun the glasses and experience could be, and encourage customers to approach the buying experience playfully and socially.

The result

The company achieved its desired results across multiple categories. It saw dramatic increases in brand awareness, engagement, cart size, conversion rate, lifetime value and reductions in time to second purchase. Overall, Zenni saw rises in campaign ROI as well, even given the increase in campaign spending.

Figure 10.4   Zenni Optical on Instagram

Table 10.5   Core metrics used

Metric	What it can show
Paid and organic traffic, social media likes, followers	Awareness and engagement of consumers
Cart size, time to purchase, loyalty and revenue potential	Revenue impact, short and long term of content initiative

SOURCE 'Content marketing performance: a framework to measure real business impact', Rebecca Lieb and Susan Etlinger, Altimeter Group (2015)

Table 10.6   Other metrics to consider

Category	Metric	What it can show
Popularity	Kudos, likes, shares, links and retweets by content unit	Which content is most popular/used
Productivity	Time to market of content-aided initiatives vs. those that are unaided	Impact of content on time to market, competitiveness, innovation

SOURCE 'Content marketing performance: a framework to measure real business impact', Rebecca Lieb and Susan Etlinger, Altimeter Group (2015)

CASE EXAMPLE

Stouffer's

The problem

Brands such as Stouffer's have traditionally relied on a mix of advertising and in-store promotions such as 'endcaps' to alert shoppers to new products or meal-planning ideas. But mobile technology changes the 'offline' shopping experience dramatically. With a mobile device and a meal-planning app (*Food on the Table*), Stouffer's has the ability to communicate with shoppers in context: while they are in the store, shopping for their next meal.[6]

The approach

While *Food on the Table* is primarily a recipe app, the reality of modern families is that preparing a full meal with side dishes is not always on the cards. In May 2014, Food on the Table and Stouffer's ran a promotion that enabled the app to suggest Stouffer's side dishes to complement recipes on the Food on the Table site.

Aside from the convenience and time-saving potential of supplementing a home-made meal, the benefit to customers is that the advertising is delivered in context, at the point of decision. A banner ad is useful insofar as it assists with unaided awareness; an in-app promotion as a consumer is making a purchase decision is far more effective.

The result

Stouffer's reported a 30–45 per cent conversion rate on products added to consumers' grocery lists in the application.

Table 10.7   Core metrics used

Metric	What it can show
Increased conversion rate	Success of the app in spurring product sales; success of digital in driving offline behaviour

SOURCE 'Content marketing performance: a framework to measure real business impact', Rebecca Lieb and Susan Etlinger, Altimeter Group (2015)

Table 10.8 Other metrics to consider

Category	Metric	What it can show
Revenue generation	[Stated] intent to purchase, leads, conversions, sales by channel, transaction size, transaction frequency. Revenue derived from owned channels compared to direct revenue, revenue by review rating. Visit loyalty Customer lifetime value	Impact of content on revenue generation, expressed in leads, intent, conversion, transaction size and frequency How content may influence revenue generation on owned channels Impact of reviews on revenue generation potential Impact of content on visit behaviour and/or customer lifetime value

SOURCE 'Content marketing performance: a framework to measure real business impact', Rebecca Lieb and Susan Etlinger, Altimeter Group (2015)

Operational efficiency

Creating enough content, efficiently and at scale within brand and production parameters, poses a substantial obstacle to many organizations – one that threatens to eat into the ROI of the content programme's own goals. At the same time, a well-calibrated content strategy can create operational efficiencies in the area of cost control, risk management and elsewhere.

CASE EXAMPLE

Unilever

The problem
For Unilever, digital marketing efforts are particularly resource intensive given its global scale, the large number of brands in its portfolio, multiple agency partners, and regional variances in support and expertise (see Figure 10.5).

Figure 10.5   Unilever's global content challenge

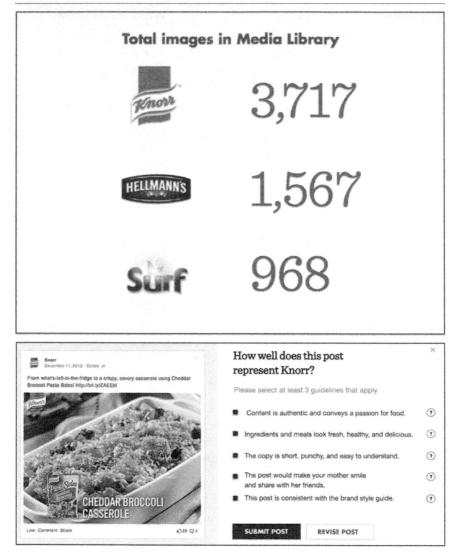

SOURCE   Percolate [Online] https://percolate.com/customers/unilever

On Facebook alone, Unilever has hundreds of millions of fans, over 1,000 people involved in the content process, and over 360 new posts daily. Creating efficiencies, brand consistency and effectiveness on a truly global scale while simultaneously managing operational costs are obvious, as well as formidable, challenges.[7]

The approach

Unilever partnered with content marketing platform Percolate in a pilot programme to attempt to create global content marketing efficiencies across three brands: Knorr, Hellman's and Surf. Teams were trained on the platform, and both global and local KPIs were established.

All content, design, local specifications and publishing are centralized in one governed environment. Global images are hosted centrally, easily accessible by all teams. Key features of this campaign included brand prompts prior to publishing; a centralized dashboard tool for calendar and creation, as well as communication and feedback; shared, customizable assets; and customized metrics linked to KPIs with visual data displays.

The result

Unilever experienced reduced time to create and publish content, and increased output (significantly, in some markets). Investing in collaborative tools to scale content globally over more than 30 brands, 40 agencies and 20 different markets has coordinated activities while reducing costs per post. (This translates to an estimated $10 million in annual savings if applied across the entire organization.) Based on these efficiencies, Unilever increased implementation by 300 per cent more licences and now operates in approximately 80 countries across 40 brands.

Table 10.9 Core metrics used

Metric	What it can show
Increased content output	Efficiency; ability to reach audiences in digital rather than analogue (phone) channels
Time to publish	Efficiency; potential for better responsiveness and cost savings
Cost per post	Productivity

SOURCE 'Content marketing performance: a framework to measure real business impact', Rebecca Lieb and Susan Etlinger, Altimeter Group (2015)

Table 10.10   Business metrics and insights

Business Goal	Business Metrics and Insights	Raw Metrics
Marketing Optimization	Increased content output Time to publish Reduction in cost per post ROI: Revenue, conversions, leads per dollar spent compared to traditional programmes ROI: Revenue, conversions, leads by content unit Time-of-day trends; best time to post Top content influencers	Which topics, brands, platforms are most successful in terms of user engagement Day-parting analysis by content unit DMP spent on SEO, content unit Most active/followed by campaign, channel, content unit Retweets, likes, fans, followers by channel Revenue, conversions, leads by channel Sentiment by channel Sentiment by influencer Sentiment, retweets, likes, fans, followers, pins by content unit Visit loyalty by content Visit loyalty/view-/click-through by channel
Revenue Generation	How content drives consideration, decision, revenue generation Drivers of reviews and ratings Impact of reviews on revenue Which channels are most effective for driving revenue	[Stated] intent to purchase Leads, conversions/sales by channel Revenue by product by channel over time Revenue by review rating Revenue derived from owned channels compared to direct revenue Traffic from paid and organic search and referral Transaction size, frequency, customer lifetime value Visit loyalty

Customer experience

Content can demonstrate value not just in attracting leads and increasing sales, but also in the realm of customer support and service, a significant cost centre in most organizations.

CASE EXAMPLE

Sony online community

The problem
According to a case study provided by Nico Henderijckx, European community and forum manager for Sony, the company's European call-centre staff found themselves repeatedly helping customers to troubleshoot a specific issue with a certain model TV set. Each call cost the brand €7.12.

The approach
According to Henderijckx, one of the company's volunteer customer forum super-users wrote a how-to troubleshooting post addressing the issue and outlining a solution. The post cost Sony nothing (as it was written by a volunteer), but was visited by 42,000 visitors in the first two weeks it was live. Leveraging data around who was interacting with this specific piece of content not only helped Sony to identify the need for similar creative content but also helped affix value to it (see Table 10.11).

The result
A call to the call centre costs the brand €7. So, the monetary value of this one post in just a fortnight was €294,000 (€7 x 42,000). Roughly translated, that's $350,000. In this case, internal, cross-departmental communication about content needs was as essential to ROI as was identifying the specific type of content to address a customer problem.

Table 10.11   Other metrics to consider

Category	Metric	What it can show
Productivity/ Cost Savings	Call deflection	Percentage of inquiries per channel that are resolved by content rather than 1–1 interaction

SOURCE 'Content marketing performance: a framework to measure real business impact', Rebecca Lieb and Susan Etlinger, Altimeter Group (2015)

Table 10.12   Core metrics used

Metric	What it can show
Call deflection	Efficiency; potential cost savings

SOURCE 'Content marketing performance: a framework to measure real business impact', Rebecca Lieb and Susan Etlinger, Altimeter Group (2015)

Table 10.13   Other metrics to consider

Category	Metric	What it can show
Popularity	Kudos, likes, shares, links and retweets by content unit	Which content is most popular/used
Potential issues/red flags	Most frequent questions online versus in call centres	Trending issues and topics that may require resolution; 'early warning system'

SOURCE 'Content marketing performance: a framework to measure real business impact', Rebecca Lieb and Susan Etlinger, Altimeter Group (2015)

Innovation

Content can be an extremely effective and efficient way to solicit ideas and engagement from community members and contribute to multiple organizational objectives.

CASE EXAMPLE

Domino's

The problem

Domino's Australia wanted to find a way to engage consumers to create their own pizza ideas, even to the point of compensating them for sales of pizzas they designed.[8]

The approach

To that end, they began a campaign in 2014 Called 'Pizza Mogul', with the tagline: 'Create. Share. Earn.'[9] The concept was simple: customers could log in to the Pizza Mogul site, create a pizza, share it, and earn money on its sales. According to the *Wall Street Journal*, one pizza designer earned roughly 32,000 Australian dollars ($27,800) from his contribution.

The concept was successful in Australia, but FTC rules governing sponsored content may prohibit US companies from launching similar programmes.

The result

Domino's Australia quantified its results simply: which were the most popular pizzas, and who earned the most from their recipes? (See Figure 10.6.) The clever twist to this strategy was that the KPIs in themselves made for interesting content, which may also have spurred continued interest.

Figure 10.6   Case example: Domino's pizzas

Table 10.14   Core metrics used

Metric	What it can show
Top-earning pizzas	Impact of content on revenue/innovation: which ideas actually generate the most revenue
Top earning customers	Impact of content on revenue/innovation: which customers benefitted most from the innovation; which could become potential advocates or influences for the brand

SOURCE 'Content marketing performance: a framework to measure real business impact', Rebecca Lieb and Susan Etlinger, Altimeter Group (2015)

Table 10.15   Other metrics to consider

Category	Metric	What it can show
Productivity	Time to market	Whether content strategies aid in time to market
Content popularity	Acceleration and reach of content over time, Popularity and sharing of content	Whether campaigns reach new audiences, which resonate, which are most shared

SOURCE 'Content marketing performance: a framework to measure real business impact', Rebecca Lieb and Susan Etlinger, Altimeter Group (2015)

Measuring by business goal

Very frequently the biggest challenge in measurement is not deciding what to measure; it is deciding what *not* to measure. Even a cursory glance at these lists of possible metrics, which admittedly is not an exhaustive list, can easily make the head spin.

But to get to a strategic approach to measurement, the first column (business goal) should drive the questions to be asked in the second column (business metrics and insights), which narrows the range of possibilities in the third column (raw metrics).

Prioritizing these goals, questions and metrics is also key, based on factors such as business value, reliability of the data, resource required to collect and analyse it, and so on.

Figure 10.7 Mapping volume metrics to business metrics

Business Goal	Business Metrics and Insights	Raw Metrics
Brand Health	Who talks about your brand, product, content	Accelerating keywords, volume, sentiment
	What people talk about regarding your brand, products, content	Change in sentiment tone and drivers
	Where people talk about your brand, products, content	Click-through rate (CTR) by content unit
	When people talk about your brand, products, content	Day-parting analysis by topic or content unit
	Why people talk about your brand, products, content	Highest-performing topics, brands, regions, by content unit
	How people talk about your brand, products, content (context)	Influencers by topic (by followers and/or reach)
		Number of fans/followers, brand mentions by content unit
		Page views/visit
		Sentiment by channel
		Sentiment by influencer
		Sentiment over time
		Social Share of Voice (SSOV) over time/vs. competitors', industry, product, topic, content unit
		Source of positive, negative, neutral sentiment
		Top keywords
		Top shared, liked, RTed, pinned, favourited, etc

SOURCE 'Content marketing performance: a framework to measure real business impact', Rebecca Lieb and Susan Etlinger, Altimeter Group (2015)

Figure 10.8 Marketing optimization and revenue generation metrics

Business Goal	Business Metrics and Insights	Raw Metrics
Marketing Optimization	Increased content output	Which topics, brands, platforms are most successful in terms of user engagement
	Time to publish	Day-parting analysis by content unit
	Reduction in cost per post	DMP spent on SEO, content unit
	ROI: Revenue, conversions, leads per dollar spent compared to traditional programmes	Most active/followed by campaign, channel, content unit
	ROI: Revenue, conversions, leads by content unit	Retweets, likes, fans, followers by channel
	Top content influencers	Revenue, conversions, leads by channel
		Sentiment by channel
		Sentiment by influencer
		Sentiment, retweets, likes, fans, followers, pins by content unit
		Visit loyalty by content
		Visit loyalty/view-/click-through by channel
Revenue Generation	How content drives consideration, decision, revenue generation	[Stated] intent to purchase
	Drivers of reviews and ratings	Leads, conversions/sales by channel
	Impact of reviews on revenue	Revenue by product by channel over time
	Which channels are most effective for driving revenue	Revenue by review rating
		Revenue derived from owned channels compared to direct revenue
		Traffic from paid and organic search and referral
		Transaction size, frequency, customer lifetime value
		Visit loyalty

SOURCE 'Content marketing performance: a framework to measure real business impact', Rebecca Lieb and Susan Etlinger, Altimeter Group (2015)

Figure 10.9 Operational efficiency, customer experience and innovation metrics

Business Goal	Business Metrics and Insights	Raw Metrics
Operational Efficiency	How digital content can reduce operating expenses by deflecting human interaction to digital interaction Drivers of service issues Possible leading indicators of risk, crisis Savings per post; useful to build a business case	Kudos, likes, shares, retweets by content unit Most frequent questions on ine versus in call centres Percentage of inquiries per channel that were resolved by content rather than 1–1 interaction
Customer Experience	How digital content can reduce operating expenses by deflecting human interaction to digital interaction	Number of service issues resolved using digital versus service interactions
Innovation	Speed to market New product ideas: owned content sparking earned content	Acceleration and reach of content over time Participation in calls to action for feedback Popularity and sharing of content

SOURCE 'Content marketing performance: a framework to measure real business impact', Rebecca Lieb and Susan Etlinger, Altimeter Group (2015)

Content measurement recommendations

Measurement must be the foundational principle of content strategy

In fact, there is no content strategy without a measurement strategy. Before embarking on a content initiative, irrespective of medium or platform, it is important to know what you want to achieve. Is it to drive more awareness? Build an audience? Encourage people to convert? Reduce call-centre expense by deflecting appropriate queries to a digital channel? Each requires different metrics – for content, yes, but also to calculate whether you have achieved your goal. Set and prioritize goals and desired outcomes, develop KPIs to track these, and measure and iterate constantly.

Every measurement strategy must focus on business outcome

Content metrics can be notoriously volume- or vanity-based, rather than outcome-based. This means that counting likes, shares or organic reach, in and of itself, likely doesn't demonstrate business value. To do that, you need to show a business outcome, using the compass in Figure 10.1 at the beginning of this chapter. For example:

- An increase in reach can show audience growth.
- An increase in shares (preferably combined with other measures of engagement) can show engagement.
- To understand whether a content strategy has affected brand reputation, you must have a benchmark, and measure sentiment, and look at the before and after. It is critical to have an analyst who can perform this correlation with an eye to other confounding factors. For example, a 'viral' video may be immensely popular, but if there is a product recall, pricing change or other factors, it may be difficult or even impossible to assess the impact on the business overall.

Know your metrics and your data

Some signals, such as click-through rate, are clear and relatively easy to assess. Measuring sharing behaviour requires that an analyst assess multiple platforms – Facebook, Twitter, Pinterest, Instagram, and others – to define what 'sharing' actually means. Compounding this issue is the fact that some of the most valuable data, for example, private Facebook data, is not available for privacy reasons. So analysts must take that into account as they assess impact, and create defensible benchmarks as part of their process.

Be realistic about organizational capabilities and tools

Because content performance data comes in a variety of shapes and sizes, from various platforms, it often requires a great deal of manual intervention to analyse properly. This is simply a reality of the market today; content vendors often supply their own analytics dashboards, while social media tools also serve to measure content reach, resonance and other (content-specific) outcomes.

It is not uncommon to require a mixture of web analytics, content measurement, marketing technology and social media tools to assess the impact of content. As a result, content strategists should work with their analysts to develop a realistic (near-term) and aspirational (longer term) measurement strategy. Otherwise, content strategists and business leaders will inevitably become frustrated, while analysts will burn out from all the manual work needed to deliver reports.

Notes

1 Rapt Media (2016) [accessed 6 January 2017] The Future of Content Report: Measuring Content Performance, *Rapt Media*. [Online] http://info.raptmedia.com/future-of-content/measuring-content-performance

2 McCain, L (2014) [accessed 6 January 2017] Winning Your Social Community: A Seattle Seahawks Case Study, *Simply Measured* [Online] http://simplymeasured.com/blog/2014/09/04/winning-your-social- community-a-seattle-seahawks-case-study/

3 '50% of Rokenbok's Customers are Generated from YouTube', see Etlinger, S (2012) [accessed 6 January 2017] The Social Media ROI Cookbook: Six Ingredients Top Brands Use to Measure the Revenue Impact of Social Media, *Altimeter Group* [Online] http://dev.altimeter group.com/2012/07/the-social-media-roi-cookbook-how-brands-measure-the-revenue-impact-of-social-media/ (see also

Kaushik, A (2016) [accessed 6 January 2017] Occam's Razor [Online] http://www.kaushik.net/avinash/)

4   WPromote (2015) [accessed 10 March 2015] Developing Zenni Optical's Social Customer Service with Content Marketing, *Wpromote* [Online] http://www.wpromote.com/clients/case-studies/content-zenni

5   The Zenni Blog (2014) [accessed 6 January 2017] Catching the Last Rays – and Looking Good Doing It!, *Zenni Blog* [Online] http://blog.zennioptical.com/catching-last-rays

6   Zaleski, D (2013) [accessed 6 January 2017] How Stouffer's Took Shopper Marketing to a New Level, *iMedia Connection* [Online] http://www.imediaconnection.com/content/34573.asp#multiview

7   Hamel, M (2015) [accessed 6 January 2017] Establishing Global Brand Consistency, *Percolate* [Online] http://percolate.com/clients/unilever

8   Griswold, A (2014) [accessed 6 January 2017] Domino's Pizza Has Handed Its Menu Over to the Internet, *Slate* [Online] http://www.slate.com/blogs/moneybox/2014/11/03/dominos_pizza_mogul_crowdsource_your_ own_pizza_toppings_combination.html

9   Domino's (2015) [accessed 6 January 2017] Pizza Mogul, *Domino's* [Online] http://www.dominos.com.au/menu/pizza-mogul

Contextual campaigns

11

'The right message to the right person at the right time.'

Digital marketing's original promise, once so bold and full of hope, is beginning to seem quaintly outdated. Marketers are now empowered to deliver context, ie content that is finely honed by a myriad of hyper-relevant factors that take critical and previously very disparate elements and data into account. This enables new levels of relevance, for example: location, real time, conditions (eg weather, sales and promotions, inventory, etc), product or service performance, product interaction, or purchase and transaction history (see Figure 11.1).

The result is far-reaching value for brands as well as their customers and prospects. Benefits and opportunities include greater return on investment (ROI), rich customer data and better customer experience. Context also can aid and facilitate lines of business beyond marketing, including (but not limited to) customer service, supply chain/distribution, CRM and product development, innovation, operations, even finance.

For these reasons, contextual marketing will soon enter a period of rapid growth and adoption. Consumers will very soon come to expect contextual communications and experiences, regardless of whether they are in a bricks-and-mortar location or using a connected device. Brands must begin now to rise to this challenge, adopting a test-and-learn approach to determine where the benefits and value of contextual marketing lie, for their own businesses, their ecosystem partners, and the benefit of their customers and prospects.

Figure 11.1   Contextual campaign – Definition

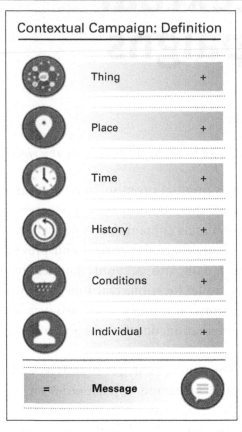

SOURCE 'Contextual campaigns: content, context and consumer connections in a post-screen world', Rebecca Lieb (2015)

Contextual campaigns: definition

Contextual marketing provides content, experiences and/or information that serve an immediate and circumstantially relevant purpose. It is 'phygital', bridging digital and physical worlds. Its scope often goes beyond traditional interfaces, such as screens (see Figure 11.1). Finally, the resultant data can inform and benefit business functions beyond marketing, as well as ecosystem partners. Contextual marketing, in short, opens a world of possibilities that do not exist with one-way marketing or advertising.

Drivers and trends

Contextual marketing, as stated above, goes both beyond the screen and blasts far beyond 'the right message to the right person at the right time'. The primary contextual drivers are set out below.

Digital pervasiveness

Sometimes termed 'phygital', contextual content and experiences are what bridge the physical and digital worlds. The convergence of embedded sensors, networked services, mobile and cloud technology – often coined as the internet of things (IoT) – means that any 'thing' can now simultaneously have a digital and physical life cycle. From wearables such as watches and clothes, to in-home appliances and entertainment systems, to (connected) cars, fobs, beacons, even in-store infrastructure, sensors and connectivity are pervading the physical world.

Example

Marantz's connected audio speakers enable the manufacturer to understand how its customers use the product. They know where the product resides, how often it is turned on and off, and what music is played from which streaming services. The company uses this data for proactive customer service, as well as for cross-sell and upsell campaigns – to great effect. 'We absolutely, 100 per cent have evidence that these targeted campaigns have a 5–7 per cent purchase rate on all the e-mails we send. The e-mail is so targeted that our open rates are 40–42 per cent', says Scott Strickland, D+M Group's global chief information officer.

The five Ws

Journalists have traditionally asked 'Who, What, When, Where and Why?' Contextual demands the same, which is why 'the right time' is only one component of potential context in contextual messaging and campaigns. Saturday evening at 8 pm may be an indicator of free time, but the 'where' (cinema, bar, restaurant, airport, electronics store or home) adds an enormous layer of additional context to temporal information for potential messaging. So do number of visits, purchase history, product interaction, proximity, weather, news, and a host of other factors.

Example

Disney resort guests receive a MagicBand, which functions as a park pass, credit card for concessions, room key and more, via thousands of sensors embedded throughout the park and hundreds of connected back-end systems. Customers can be greeted by name at park attractions, shop, or order food at restaurants that 'finds' them at their table. Another feature is, as Disney's SVP for direct to consumer, Gunjan Bhow, puts it: 'Using my data in terms of line length, and capacity, to make my day more magical, entertaining, delightful. If a customer is waiting in a particularly long line, based on the context of what you have done in your day, and how long different lines are, we can present to you a preferable line with the notification: "There's only a two-minute line at Alice in Wonderland." We also get tremendous customer engagement, app downloads and word of mouth.'

Product as real-time brand extension

Products and infrastructure become a real-time extension of the brand. Through sensors/data and content, they provide brands with an opportunity to touch customers more often and more relevantly.

Example

The MyQ garage door opener alerts users if they left their house open and vulnerable, and also sends garage door activity alerts so homeowners can track comings and goings.

Shift from cookie-based to individual targeting

Cookie-based targeting has long been in decline,[1] due to the fact that cookies are tied to devices rather than to individuals (and many of those individuals delete cookies). Targeting specific consumers, independent of device via CRM, loyalty, proximity or other data is an essential element of contextual marketing.

Smartphone adoption

Increasingly, consumers' smartphones are likely to have Wi-Fi, GPS, NFC, RFID, accelerometers, cameras, microphones, BLE, iBeacon and other interactive features turned on, the latter function estimated at 40 per cent and growing.[2] These features are essential for enabling contextual marketing. Because phones are all but expected to communicate with wearables, gaming, home devices, within retail, and automobiles, younger consumers especially are entering an always-on mode in terms of these features,[3] making them reachable. A Mobile First strategy means leveraging the sensors in mobile hardware; smartphones are the remote control for everything.

Infrastructure adoption

Retailers and location-based businesses are rushing to embrace contextual technology such as embedded sensors, beacons, geofencing, and Wi-Fi. Adoption of devices has, and will continue, to surge[4] – with 6.2 million proximity sensors in use in spring 2016. Additionally, IoT, smart packaging and other devices are on a similar growth curve.

Customer journey/customer experience

Interest and attention to the customer journey, across channels and media, and throughout the purchase funnel, has spiked in recent years. According to Google Trends,[5] searches for the term have increased by a factor of 20 over the past 12 years. Contextual marketing will soon be an essential tool for keeping track of customers across devices, locations and purchase cycle.

Decreasing ad effectiveness

As traditional banner ads plummet in efficacy,[6] marketers remain continually challenged to reach consumers with messaging that is relevant, useful, persuasive, or that creates engagement, particularly on mobile platforms that lack the 'real estate' for display advertising. Context is a powerful tool in the new marketing arsenal that is far less paid media-centric.

The integration imperative

Context in marketing cannot exist without closely integrated software systems. Disney's MagicBand relies on over 100 backend systems. That APIs are now standard with most software systems creates the ability to connect people, places and things. Systems, networks, security and devices are increasingly interoperative.

Contextual marketing: the rewards

Contextual marketing is complex, requires significant upfront investment and a reimagining of strategy. Why bother? Marketers who test the waters quickly become committed for a myriad of factors (see Figure 11.2), with ROI, higher sales and profitability topping the list of potential rewards to marketers, as well as benefits that go well beyond sales and marketing to functions such as sales, service and retention.

Financial

ROI: Disney's Gunjan Bhow puts it bluntly: 'The more context there is, the more ROI.' Disney recouped the R&D costs of tying in video pre-order campaigns with geofenced in-theatre and in-store promotions (with partners including Fandango and Walmart) in less than six months with only three such promotions. As mentioned earlier, Marantz is currently seeing a phenomenal 5–7 per cent purchase rate on e-mail campaigns targeted by IoT data from speakers.

Targeted marketing

Campaign and sales effectiveness

IoT products provide visibility into customer channel affinity, leading to more effective media buys. Using deep customer data to understand who buys, and under what circumstances (eg sales-motivated, new features, etc), enables manufacturers to reduce inventory, lower write-offs and not sell at huge discounts. Because real time is a factor

Figure 11.2   Contextual Campaign – Ecosystem of Value

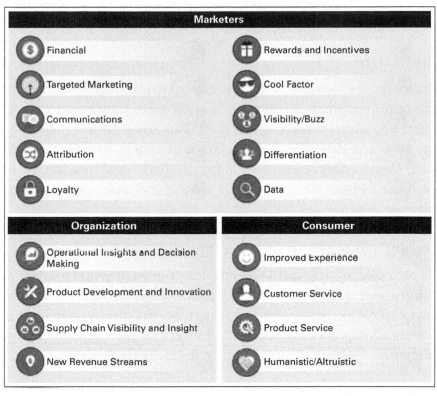

SOURCE 'Contextual campaigns: content, context and consumer connections in a post-screen world', Rebecca Lieb (2015)

in most contextual campaigns, promotions can easily be designed to craft special offers and/or service to move excess inventory, eg food in a restaurant or empty theatre seats.

Precise targeting

Integrating data sets such as CRM, purchase history and psycho-profiles results in surgically precise targeting, enabling marketers to craft offers that are far more compelling than those in broader-based initiatives.

Communication opportunities

Innovations such as smart packaging (eg NFC-enabled) can provide information beyond the label at point-of-purchase such as freshness or additional nutrition data. This can build trust and provide a nudge towards purchase at the point of decision, of interest to major CPG brands such as Nestlé. Contextual campaigns can also monitor use or conditions to alert consumers when to purchase or service a product, and/or provide news, updates or public awareness.

Attribution

Because contextual campaigns are targeted to individuals who largely opt-in to participate, attribution is much more transparent than in more traditional marketing channels. This has a twofold effect: 1) opt-in is user-driven (campaigns must, of course, provide value to users) and consent is actively obtained; 2. the real-time nature of such campaigns offers consumers context for understanding what they opt-in to.

Loyalty

By providing value, experiences and an opt-in relationship contextual campaigns can foster loyalty or become critical drivers of existing customer loyalty programmes. In effect, brands can leverage sensors and data integrations to reward consumers for their behaviours and interactions with the brand, product, in-store experience, etc.

Rewards and incentives

Direct and highly contextual messaging can spur purchase and reward users for their actions. Taco Bell has partnered with Waze, for example, to incentivize nearby drivers to make a late-night purchase and receive a free dessert with their order. An iPhone app created by Dentsu in Japan allows shoppers to see animated butterflies flitting by. Each butterfly contains a coupon for a nearby business.

Cool factor

Both Hollister and MGM Resorts are looking to Snapchat as a branding initiative, serving relevant content when customers are near a physical location. 'Is it moving the needle?' asks Andy Kennemer of Abercrombie & Fitch: 'It makes us cool and relevant. We're doing it because it feels right', he says, adding that the app is highly mobile, as well as highly social for teens.

Visibility and buzz

Earned media – social, PR and word of mouth – are frequent byproducts of contextual marketing initiatives. This halo effect will continue for the next two years, while contextual campaigns continue to enjoy a novelty value. When Unilever's Maille Dijon mustard-targeted foodie consumers in supermarkets with beacons, the initiative garnered national media attention.

Differentiation

In addition to sparking consumer engagement in lower-interest categories (eg soft drinks, CPG), contextual marketing is a differentiator with partners ranging from online to bricks-and-mortar retail locations. Both manufacturers and retailers can, for example, benefit from joint campaigns as well as the resultant data.

Data 360° view of customer

General location and hyper-local proximity are just two examples of a wealth of new customer data and customer journey information opened up by contextual marketing. DealerOn's Greg Gifford, director of search and social, for example, intends to use beacon data to learn which customers visit automobile dealerships for service versus those who might be interested in buying, by tracking their movements inside the building. Additionally, some dealers are interested in targeting browsers who visit the lot when the dealership is closed. Triangulated with data from purchase history, Facebook and other social networks, or the large ad networks, this richer data feeds into a wealth of potential messaging and CRM initiatives.

Deeper customer data

When provided with information and experiences that are valuable, useful, fun or interesting, consumers will, in exchange, volunteer more data and information. In fact, the more devices consumers own, the more interested they are in engaging with brands about the use of their data.[7]

Context beyond third-party data

Ultimately, brands may need to invest less in third-party data and targeting once highly contextual data streams are established. This deeper, proprietary data can in some cases itself be productized (see 'New revenue streams' later in this chapter).

Benefits for the organization

Operational insights and decision making

How customers interact with brands before, during and after their purchase experiences carries insights far beyond marketing. Many brands are implementing in-store technologies, for example, not to immediately engage shoppers, but instead taking initial steps towards tracking store traffic, layout and inventory. While foot patterns can be used for marketing optimization, brands are also (often initially to 'test the waters' of such new technology) using this data for back-end operational decision making involving stock, labour allocations, in-store layout, energy efficiencies, employee communications, governance, etc.

Product development and innovation

Contextual information from campaigns and devices feeds back into R&D and helps to maximize investment. Manufacturers can retire features they know customers are not using, and develop new products targeted to who their customers are and how products are used. D+M noticed, for example, that a large number of customers named their audio gear 'Bathroom', so they developed a waterproof line to market to those consumers, which quickly sold out. A more rugged line of products is currently in development for customers who name their set-up 'Garage'.

Supply chain visibility and insight

Contextual marketing, sensors and IoT functionality provide visibility into how products are used, and shine new light on the supply chain and distribution. Nestlé hopes, for example, to soon only dispatch its delivery fleet to stock freezers that are empty, bypassing retailers not short on inventory. And, as one manufacturer we interviewed put it, 'If you know where products are you can recall them if necessary.' Smart packaging on CPG products, while potentially providing unique social media tie-ins or access to exclusive content for consumers, also offers manufacturers insights about patterns and integrity of the distribution and/or retail life cycle.

New revenue streams

Manufacturers that embed connectivity capabilities into products are amassing significant data about how consumers use and interact with those devices, as well as the services they connect to those devices. 'IT could become a profit centre', notes one executive we spoke with: 'We are considering selling this data back to streaming media services, for example, so they can directly see how they stack up against their competitors.' Partnerships across distributors, manufacturers, vendors, retailers, telecom, insurance and a diverse array of other service providers also introduce new business model opportunities through connected product data.

Benefits for consumers

Improved experience

Contextual experiences can surprise, delight, assist, inform and entertain consumers, leading in turn to increased loyalty, word of mouth and brand favourability.

Customer service

Implanted IoT technology allows manufacturers to proactively offer customer service when, for example, a device has been restarted numerous times within a specific time frame, indicating the consumer may be having issues or requires assistance. The opportunity is both enhancing reactive support as well as enabling proactive (and eventually predictive) support.

Product service

Smart devices can 'phone home' to automatically upgrade or, for example, order supplies. A printer might be connected to Amazon or Staples to automatically replenish its ink. The ability for products (such as Amazon's Echo) not only to serve as platforms for content and services, but increase in functionality, personalization and value over time through software updates, is a disruptive customer relationship model.

Humanistic/altruistic

Contextual marketing can not only spur or assist in purchases, conversions and transactions, but also genuinely help consumers by, for example, monitoring their health and making suggestions for care or remedies for underserved populations such as the elderly or blind.

Contextual marketing: the risks

As with any new form of marketing and emerging marketing technology, contextual campaigns bring risks together with benefits. While risks can be mitigated with best practices, which are also still emerging, it is important they be carefully considered by brands embarking into contextual campaigns and messaging.

Given below are the primary risks that marketers say they are encountering.

Creepiness

Deep visibility into what consumers are doing, where they are when, and what things they are using or interacting with can shock, jar and otherwise come across as Big Brotherish when contextual communications are read as overpersonalized.

Alienating users

False positives, bad data and incorrectly configured campaigns can result in undesired effects. A nearby consumer who hates a brand might be targeted with a message from that brand. Poor profiling can damage brand credibility.

Differing privacy and data laws

Brands operating on a global scale must often tailor contextual campaigns regionally due to differing laws and regulations around data, privacy and data sharing with partners. Upcoming regulations such as the Global Data Protection Regulation (GDPR) could fundamentally alter how organizations can collect, store and analyse customer data in specific countries. Mandates such as this will have a direct impact on businesses' requirements around obtaining consent, profiling, data protection, cyber-security, certifications, etc. Cultural variations and sensitivities will also be a consideration.

Opt-in and permission requirements

To operate at scale, brands will be challenged to effectively communicate value to consumers, otherwise they will risk being shut out or ignored.

Bad data

Brands must keep multiple data sources current in order to maintain and ensure context. When a retail location moves, for example, incorrect location data may be the result.

Investment

Contextual marketing can still be expensive, not only in terms of data and enterprise technology investments, but also deployment on a mass scale. 'Thin film [packaging] applications create new opportunities to engage at point-of-purchase', notes Nestlé's Mark Brodeur, global head of digital marketing innovation. 'But currently the cost is still out of reach at scale as we sell approximately 1.2 billion units per day around the globe.'

Customer adoption and scale

Highly dependent on category, for some brands – such as clothing retailers where an average customer shops only three or four times annually – it can be difficult to justify investment. Another aspect is how many customers will be detectable in the environment via Bluetooth, Wi-Fi or shared location.

Inevitable tragedy of the commons

All new forms of digital marketing technology have brought with their benefits the potential for abuse, exploitation and malpractice. Irresponsible and unethical marketers will inevitably tar contextual marketing with that brush, arousing consumer suspicion and potential regulatory attention.

Attribution

While contextual campaign attribution exceeds that of more traditional advertising, multi-touch attribution is still not mature and can be a stumbling block. Connect this back to the need for systems and device interoperability. Otherwise we are just creating more silos. This also calls forth integration across 'domains' – home, car, work, in-store, etc.

Culture and teams

Establishing and scaling teams, marrying marketing and technology, education, standards and measurement remain uncharted territory in many organizations.

Lack of content strategy

Though we have discussed at length in this book the importance of a foundational content strategy, the preponderance of brands are still lacking one. Overwhelmingly, mindsets remain both campaign- and product-centric. Contextual campaigns require a wealth of content that is contextually and channel relevant, personalized but not creepy, and in numerous versions that address multiple scenarios (time, locations, conditions, device, etc).

Interoperability and integration

Walled-garden media channels and a lack of fully integrated back-end systems that seamlessly integrate CRM, data, creative, advertising, social media and a host of other marketing and enterprise functions limit campaign efficacy, as well as marketers' views of the individuals interacting with the campaign.

Novelty factor

As with other emerging technologies that were once marketing darlings, campaign efficacy may fall off after the initial novel effect, dampening marketers' faith and enthusiasm. The utility and real value creation (versus noise) of such campaigns becomes central to their viability and reception.

Strategically planning contextual campaigns

Overwhelmingly, marketers committed to contextual campaigns extol the rewards and potential of the practice, while at the same time emphasizing the complexities of the inherent considerations. Given below are the primary considerations that marketers must consider before investing in context.

What comes first: technology, data or the consumer?

The primary differentiator in approach to contextual marketing seems to be the chicken-and-egg(s) question of what drives campaigns: technology innovation, the customer journey or data.

Marketer approaches at this point seem to largely rest on the size and diversity of the business. Smaller, more vertically driven businesses are more likely to say 'it also rests completely on the technology' – the approach of DealerOn's Greg Gifford.

Other marketers cite specific vision and the ability to solve problems or optimize performance as an impetus. Triangulating first, third and partner data to target in-store coupons and map online/offline conversion is one example. One retailer (who asks not to be identified) found the SKUs selling on the company's app were not moving in physical stores. This sales and behavioural data led to a change in the physical merchandising strategy. Yext CMO Jeffrey Rohrs emphasizes that you must first define the outcome you are seeking before you can map the 'story' that will lead customers through content and technology.

The largest, most diversified enterprises view tech as 'table stakes', as GE's Andrew Markowitz puts it, looking instead at a broader corporate vision: 'Tech makes all things possible, but it doesn't necessarily make them easier', he notes. Nestlé's approach is similar, considering brand DNA and 'why are we in business' before technology, the latter of which Mark Brodeur calls 'an enabler'.

The most mature companies will lead strategy with customer journey and experience, as well as a value exchange between brand and customer. Technology and data support that vision and its execution.

Partners and ecosystem

Internal partnerships

Contextual campaigns require significant integration of disparate technologies, data sources and partnerships among stakeholders. Internal alignment is critical at the enterprise level between, for example, marketing and IT, as well as among any functions embracing CRM and data. Legal must also have a seat at the table where data and privacy are concerned. Similarly, MGM Resort's Beverly Jackson also cites security's role in campaigns tied to physical locations. Operations can help keep locations' data current.

External partnerships

Contextual campaigns also require rethinking external partnerships. For manufacturers, this can necessitate finding retail partners willing to experiment with in-store technologies such as beacons and sensors, with both parties sharing responsibility, investment, insights and data. Disney looks to partnerships with cinema chains and online partners such as Fandango and YouTube in order to target customers when they are seeing a film. The customer journey breadcrumb trail of where and what a customer has clicked on reveals more useful data, according to Disney's Bhow, than a customer's interaction directly with the brand or its products: 'The big revelation is that your journey as a person is far more useful for us than even the Disney journey you took.'

Market information and data services from NPD Group, Nielsen, JD Power and similar suppliers, as well as point-of-sale data, are also frequently critical to shape and inform contextual campaigns. When context and intelligence in the form of technology are embedded into objects, these partnerships extend to technology providers, designers and manufacturers.

While agencies don't yet figure prominently in the partnership equation for contextual campaigns, when they do it is likely to be the consultancies now competing in the agency space, eg Accenture and Deloitte. As one brand executive put it, 'These initiatives require so much systems integration that agencies just put up their hands and leave. They only want to know what media to buy.'

It is expected that the equation of hardware manufacturer/agency dependence will shift in three to five years as momentum increases. So too will the landscape of vendors, creating too many point systems for brands to keep track of, as well as more end-to-end solutions and evolution in standards, APIs and other integration capabilities.

Budgeting for contextual campaigns

Marketers are understandably reluctant to share figures regarding investment in contextual campaigns, but by all indications those who are investing are doubling down on their financial commitment to the channel.

'This is the fastest-growing part of our budget now.'

Gunjan Bhow, Walt Disney Company

Other marketers agree. The value of providing a near 360-degree view of the customer has upped one retailer's investment by a factor of 75x over the past five years. 'We're out of TV entirely', states MGM Resort's Beverly Jackson, who has more than doubled contextual investment from 30 per cent in 2015 to 64 per cent of budget in 2016, making up that increase from traditional media spend. As marketers chase millennial consumers, this trend will accelerate.

Marantz points to more effective e-mail sell rates, for example, to help justify continued campaign investment. 'But how do you amortize the cost of the platform over the campaign?' asks Scott Strickland: 'We take that generally as a capital investment', a type of accounting generally foreign to marketing and sales operations. Benefits to other lines of business (CRM, product development, service, etc) must also factor into the calculation.

Developing platforms from which campaigns can operate, as well as collect and ultimately leverage collected data, is currently the biggest investment commitment. While enterprises invest an estimated 15–20 per cent of their sandbox budgets on actual campaigns at present, infrastructure development can be a multimillion-dollar commitment, dependent on business decisions such as build, buy and/or partner.

After spending an estimated $1 billion on the MagicBand roll-out, Disney, for example, has carved out a new, multimillion-dollar budget for anticipated platform build out with partners such as Apple, Amazon and Walmart. 'These are not campaigns in the traditional sense', notes Bhow, who stresses non-marketing aspects of the initiatives such as customer experience and service.

Another important aspect impacting investment is whether contextual campaigns are long or short term. Evergreen, always-on campaigns, eg a fast-food restaurant promoting daily specials to commuters, require multimillion-dollar investments as opposed to a back-to-school promotion, which on the low end might represent $10,000–$25,000. Many brands have not yet moved beyond a test and incubate stage, committing no more than $100,000 to an initiative. 'It's a big opportunity', notes GE's Andrew Markowitz, 'but not yet a big investment.'

Other marketing channels factor into budgetary decisions. Contextual campaigns account for up to 60–70 per cent of one retail brand's marketing budget, but only if e-mail marketing costs are also factored into that budget. Otherwise, that number would be closer to 30–40 per cent – still an impressive figure.

Emerging platforms from vendors such as Xperiel will soon lower investments considerably by integrating things, devices, interfaces and information into more integrated and interoperable platforms.

Technology integrations

Any system, platform or campaign must be designed from inception with a view towards integration. As previously mentioned, a host of integrations are essential for any contextual campaign, including:

Data

Akin to integration, achieving relevant context is reliant on numerous data points (and sets), not just one or two. Data sourcing, interpretation, warehousing and safeguarding are core to contextual marketing, and not just from a customer or CRM standpoint. Other potential

Table 11.1 Technology integrations

Marketing automation	Semantic technologies	Artificial intelligence
E-mail and other messaging	Workflows and systems	Chat and service bots
CRM tools	Stakeholders and partners	NLP
Data sets	Personalization	Conversational Commerce
Content and creative assets	Localization	Machine learning
Social platforms	Attribution	Image recognition
Third-party data	Journey mapping	Cognitive computing
Listening tools	Analytics	
Smart devices	Real-time capabilities	

SOURCE 'Contextual campaigns: content, context and consumer connections in a post-screen world', Rebecca Lieb (2016)

data considerations can focus on time of day/month/year; weather; holidays; inventory; location; news, etc. All of these points can become even more granular. An auto dealership will craft messaging differently to customers in the service section of the property than those browsing vehicles on the lot, while CPG manufacturers craft offers on the shelf level.

Value exchange

Value is a concept that differs enormously by industry vertical and campaign purpose, but if there is no inherent value for the target audience, there is no reason for them to participate, or to exchange information or data with the marketers. Value can be a literal offer – eg a coupon, information, entertainment (Pokémon Go) – or a new level of convenience (REI's location-aware app offers a National Park concierge service[8]). Value must be identified at the beginning of the experience that brands drive with contextual marketing, as well as tie into campaign KPIs. This is also an ongoing effort, in which interaction data informs evaluation and re-evaluation of what we are measuring and why.

Permission/opt-in and out

Overwhelming customers with a surfeit of push messaging is anti-thetical to the concept of value. 'Not being creepy', one of the primary concerns of marketers eager to engage with contextual marketing, is contingent on communicating value so customers will opt in, and respecting the wishes of those who say no.

Content strategy

Several marketers pointed to the lack of a content strategy, or myriad versioning of content for differing contextual scenarios, as one of the most difficult yet critical aspects of planning for contextual marketing. Salesforce's Lindsey Irvine states, 'Customers' number one priority is delivering the right content, over everything else. You're going to turn off a customer if it's the wrong content at the wrong time.'

Metrics and KPIs

Contextual campaigns can be applied to a myriad of marketing (as well as other) goals. Determining what to measure can be as challenging for many marketers as developing measurement systems in an ecosystem so rife with data.

Contextual campaign aspects that can be used as KPIs include:

- Build audience;
- Increase household footprint;
- Coupon acceptance/offer redemption;
- User behaviour (eg movement through physical locations);
- Click-through;
- Increased sales;
- Point-of-purchase sales;
- Cross-selling and upselling;
- Pre-orders;
- Streamlined/proactive customer service;
- Move excess inventory;
- Cost per action or transaction;
- In-store traffic;
- Increased intelligence/data collection;
- Drive customers to other media channels (e-mail, social, etc);
- Downloads;
- Improved media buys (eg drive to contextual campaign awareness; target social media ads to consumers).

Best practices and recommendations

As campaigns move beyond what might now be considered 'traditional' devices and screens to permeate the environments we inhabit and the things we use, interact with or are even just in proximity with, marketers understandably can become somewhat overwhelmed. Technology makes more things possible, but that is not to say it makes them easier.

Best practices are emerging and mutable in any digital marketing discipline, but nowhere so much as the very nascent practice of contextual marketing. Based on our research, below is a list of emergent contextual marketing best practices.

Strategy and vision

'Definitely do it'

The overwhelming majority of marketers we spoke with who are involved in contextual campaigns are unanimous that the benefits of such initiatives are too big to ignore. Small pilot projects build understanding, process, insight and expertise.

Have a vision

Know what you want to achieve as an organization. Think creatively, beyond the technology to the Big Idea and keep the consumer point of view in mind. 'Just because we can add sensors to just about anything doesn't mean we should', explains Nestlé's Brodeur.

Start slowly

Pilot simple initiatives first, learn, then go larger while at the same time developing processes, people and teams. 'We had to create a whole new operating model around these campaigns', says Beverly Jackson, MGM Resorts: 'We sit down, agree on timeline and monitor the launch.' Consider ripple effects, such as potentially overwhelming a logistics provider in terms of shipping.

Hedge your bets

While ramping, pilot multiple initiatives. There are many areas in which contextual campaigns can succeed (marketing, supply chain, customer service, product, etc). An important part of the pilot/learn process is not to be confined to one small arena.

Data and analytics

Make data-based decisions

Understand and incorporate data into campaigns, as well as determine what are the desired data outputs. For example, what data is required to support a 360-degree customer view? What data is required to close the offer loop, making it so relevant and targeted that the deal is clinched? How do you recognize high-value customers? How will you make the leap from knowing who a customer is to knowing where that individual is and, perhaps most importantly, why?

Share data

Insights, trends and intelligence gleaned from contextual campaigns can have value that far exceeds marketing's reach. Usage data can funnel into product development, the supply chain or customer service, for example. It is critical to interpret data through many lenses and ensure insight is shared with the appropriate internal line of business or external partners.

KPIs and metrics

'Start slow' is again the rule of thumb here. DealerOn has, for example, seen up to a 46 per cent increase in click-through rates, which Greg Gifford terms 'pretty awesome'. The company aspires to but has not yet built the ability to track sales and lead lift via beacon targeting in auto dealership (and subsequent Facebook retargeting). Instead, in this pilot phase, dealers currently use the technology to build lists by encouraging car shoppers to link on social networks and subscribe to e-mail. A host of goals can be applied to contextual campaigns (see the section 'Metrics and KPIs', above). Marketers are responsible for selecting achievable, measurable goals at the outset and to build those learnings going forward.

Create unique offers and communications in different channels for tracking purposes. A beacon audience, for example, should receive a coupon, code or URL unique to that channel for proper attribution.

Triangulate multiple data sources

Geodata expert Neal Welbourne claims that none of his clients have ever been precise about who is their real customer. He recommends crunching internal data, such as CRM and past interaction history, with external sources such as Experian, Equifax and Transunion as well as social media to build the stories of the people who actually interact with products.

Move beyond insight to action

Data can provide numerous insights (eg how many people in the area are buying running shoes?). You can learn that information quickly. The key is analysis: determining what problems you can solve with that knowledge – and where opportunities can be found.

Reality check

Physical and/or environmental interaction becomes a critical factor in measurement. Numerous factors, such as weather and location, will factor into why a consumer is interacting with a mobile device. 'Marketers are so focused on who clicked that they forget what is going on', observes Neal Welbourne. As an example: 'Targeting for running shoes those runners who use treadmills in a gym in areas that have high rainfall and cold temperatures' – the outdoor runner will probably not be reachable in the rain.

Practitioner recommendations

Teams: for pilot projects, initiatives can often start with one line of business (e-mail, customer service, social or mobile) then spread through the organization. Education, knowledge sharing, agility and empowerment are essential to spark thought and experimentation.

Content strategy

Existing content strategies must be significantly expanded to address contextual campaigns. This must encompass not only goals and KPIs, which can be myriad, but also the many additional situations, conditions, offers, customer profiles conditions, locations, device interfaces and other specifics that go into communication and messaging.

Content strategy must be linked to product strategy for many contextual initiatives, and also address design and user experience to a higher degree than in other marketing scenarios.

Anticipate and script responses

The real-time nature of contextual campaigns requires outbound and inbound scenario mapping then scripting content to address numerous potential situations and reactions, both to offers as well as the campaigns themselves. When D+M, for example, is called out for being slightly creepy with proactive customer service push messaging in response to consumer behaviours with their devices, the scripted response is, 'You would expect this level of support from BMW. Why not from us?' – which the company has found to be a successful way to allay feelings of surveillance. This applies equally to potential consumer cross-domain sensitivities.

Real-time ability

Real time and context go hand in hand. Location data, for example, cannot suggest that a customer visits a venue when it is closed; iced tea is an inappropriate offer for a snow day. Follow the 12 steps to prepare for real-time readiness as outlined in Chapter 8. Many brands already have always-on war rooms in which highly trained social media and analytics teams monitor digital sentiment and interaction 24/7, reacting and optimizing messaging in real time. The sentient world will rapidly become part of this intense, pressurized marketing function.

Permission and opt-in

Even more than with e-mail and social channels, contextual communications cannot be pushed on unwilling or unreceptive consumers. In addition to offering value to make messaging welcome, permission is a critical component of the brand/consumer dialogue, as is an opt-out mechanism, especially for brands leveraging data across domains (eg in-home, -car, -store, etc). The four components of permission communications that every brand must consider include: education; brand accountability; consent and agency; and value/WIIFM (what's in it for me?).

Ecosystem of internal and external partners

Consider new partnerships, both internally and externally. Contextual campaigns touch areas beyond marketing, and the data inputs and outputs can be of value for a broad variety of stakeholders. This value can and should be used as a justification of spend, not just from marketing budgets but also from other line of business budgets.

Technology vendors

Understand what they bring to the table, as well as limitations. A large player can act as a backstop, but limit experimentation. A small, nimble start-up might be better for a pilot than a national implementation. Determine who will be responsible for the chain of technology, for example a chain of 1,000 retail locations, each with 10 beacons.

Continuous education and training

In a quickly evolving sector it is essential to keep abreast of tools, technologies, use cases, data and best practices.

The future of contextual campaigns

After the first wave of contextual marketing because it's 'cool', what's next? As with all new technologies, context currently has a high novelty-value factor. More strategic brands must ask themselves 'How will we work, play, shop, travel and interact with places and things in the future?'

Marketing's future will be based on experience, service and utility, as consumer attention becomes an ever-scarcer commodity. Content is ubiquitous. To thrive and to differentiate, brand must evolve from content to context to connection. There are five ways that brands can achieve this, singly or in combination:

- *Entertaining customer experiences*: storytelling and other forms of entertainment.

- *Deeper information*: providing knowledge, decision-making tools, etc.

- *Enhanced services*: improved customer and product services.

- *Streamlined services*: more convenience, less friction, eg mobile banking.

- *Automated services*: work almost seamlessly in the background, eg Amazon Dash.

To meet growing consumer expectations, which are evolving as quickly as the technology landscape, brands must begin not only to consider but also to experiment with how they will contextually engage with customers and prospects in the very near future.

Notes

1 Fulgoni, G (2012) [accessed 6 January 2017] When the Cookie Crumbles, *ComScore* [Online] https://www.comscore.com/Insights/Blog/When-the-Cookie-Crumbles

2 Coombs, J (2015) [accessed 6 January 2017] The Straight Goods on Bluetooth: How Many Consumers Have It On?, *Rover* [Online] http://blog.roverlabs.co/post/117195525589/the-straight-goods-on-bluetooth-how-many

3 Coombs, J (2015) [accessed 6 January 2017] The Straight Goods on Bluetooth: How Many Consumers Have It On?, *Rover* [Online] http://blog.roverlabs.co/post/117195525589/the-straight-goods-on-bluetooth-how-many

4 Jaye, K (2016) [accessed 6 January 2017] Proximity Sensors in Stores and Elsewhere Surge, New Report Suggests, *Advertising Age* [Online] http://adage.com/article/datadriven-marketing/mobile-beacons-grew-22-q4-2015/303655/

5 Google Trends (2016) [accessed 6 January 2017] Customer Journey 2004 – Present, *Google Trends* [Online] https://www.google.com/trends/explore#q=%22customer%20journey%22

6 Lieb, R (2016) [accessed 6 January 2017] The Eclipse of Online Ads, *RebeccaLieb.com* [Online] http://rebeccalieb.com/sites/default/files/downloads/The%20Eclipse%20of%20Online%20Ads%20-%20Final.pdf

7 Altimeter (2016) [accessed 6 January 2017] Consumer Perceptions of Privacy in the Internet of Things, *Prophet* [Online] http://www.

altimetergroup.com/2015/06/new-report-consumer-perceptions-of-privacy-in-the-internet-of-things/

8 Recreational Equipment, Inc (2016) [accessed 6 January 2017] REI – National Parks Guide and Maps, *iTunes* [Online] https://itunes.apple.com/us/app/rei-national-parks-guide-maps/id1031987936?mt=8

INDEX

Note: Page numbers in *italics* indicate a Figure or Table in the text.

CPSIA information can be obtained
at www.ICGtesting.com
Printed in the USA
LVOW05s2233180617
538521LV00039B/2093/P